PROBLEMS OF OUR OWN

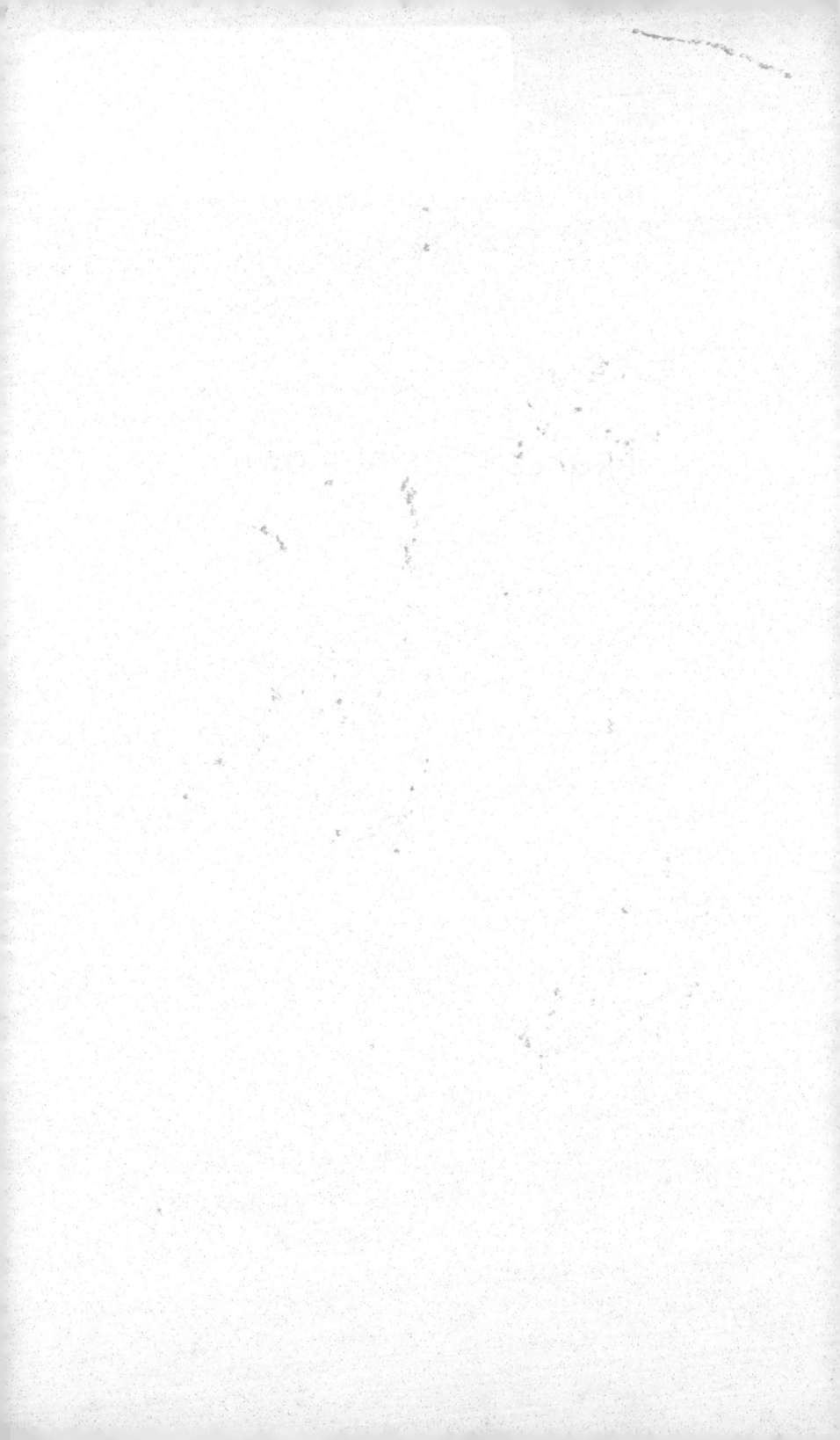

PROBLEMS OF OUR OWN

A COMING OUT STORY, TOGETHER

STEPHEN FORD

NDP

NEW DEGREE PRESS

PROBLEMS OF OUR OWN
A Coming Out Story, Together

ISBN 979-8-88504-634-3 *Paperback*
979-8-88504-952-8 *Kindle Ebook*
979-8-88504-839-2 *Ebook*

For those finding themselves

CONTENTS

———

AUTHOR'S NOTE

Growing up, I was often the target of many intentionally hateful comments that stigmatize the LGBTQ community, as in "queer," "gay," and "fag," to name a few. I realize I never actually labeled these acts as bullying in the moment. Now, I would very much categorize them as such. Those moments became monumental when it came to building myself up and loving myself—two things I never did and still struggle with.

My mental health issues derived from these moments, and though I acted as if these words were not bothersome at the time, they subconsciously were. My confidence is still redeveloping to this day.

Similarly, homophobic actions, rather than words, also create long-term discomfort in the lives of those affected. I have witnessed parents sacrifice the long-term well-being of their child by kicking them out on the streets for simply coming out as gay and telling them who they are on the inside. These actions can place youth in foster care, involve them with drugs and/or violence, or lead to suicide. It takes years for kids to recover from these types of homophobic actions.

To address the issue of society normalizing these homophobic words and actions, I wrote the following book.

I spent time rebuilding, growing, and learning through the pain rather than addressing it. Feeling like I had to constantly be someone I wasn't became exhausting and detrimental to my mental state. I'm not that person anymore. My message is this—you don't need to spend time being someone you're not.

Be yourself.

The most terrifying results I always dreamed of didn't come to fruition. In fact, I was welcomed with open arms, metaphorically applauded in many ways, and most importantly, I was happier.

In reading the following piece, reflect on how this applies directly to you. Beyond the homophobic discrimination, tap into the feelings of defeat and vulnerability. How can these feelings be taken and used in a way that helps others affected day to day by discrimination? As a society, we see discrimination every day. As a society, we should stand up for one another every day. We all fight the same fight, simply in a different light.

Many years ago, I started this journey to make me stronger. Now I know I started this journey in the hope one person will resonate with this story and stand up for what is right when those bullies attack. I wrote this book to spread the word of kindness. There is no right or wrong way to be a human, but there is a right or wrong way to treat one.

BLUE TEE

———

I'm at work when I notice a vibration in my pocket, alerting me a new text has just come through. Unable to help myself, I reach into my pocket and pull out my phone to see a text from @tarted3. My face lights up with a huge grin. Instead of continuing to cut the cheese pizzas in front of me, I delicately begin choosing what I want to say in response to the text.

My very best friend, Nellie, catches me slacking off on the job. We happen to work together at a little pizza shop that we like to call "Papa Smurf's." Her dark brown eyes widen as she sassed, "Boy are you typing a damn book? Why are you smiling so damn big?"

Wrapping up my text, my eyes slowly veer up to hers while cracking up at her reaction. I play with her emotions, replying "Nellie, this stays here if I tell you." She grows serious and invested with just this one sentence. "I'm serious. Do you promise?" I repeated. We cross pinkies, planting a kiss on them while my confidence builds enough to finally confess the secret I've been keeping to myself for a few weeks. "Nellie, I've been talking to someone."

Perking up as if we aren't at work anymore, Nellie spouts, "Wait, for real? Who? Where'd y'all meet? Do you have a picture?" Smiling, I pull out my phone and type "tarted3" in the Instagram search bar and hand over the phone. She first chooses my favorite photo of him in a blue T-shirt. She zooms in and out to see the details in his face with absolutely zero facial expression.

The suspense is killing me. My eyes anxiously dart back and forth from my phone to her face. Finally, "Bitch, why didn't you tell me you were gay? You know I don't give a shit," she says, her face finally breaking out in a smile.

Without skipping a beat, my eyes gratefully begin to water as I release a sigh of relief. "You know the luxury of simply coming out didn't exist in high school. And since we decided to stay in town for college, our high school basically followed us to the University of Cincinnati. It has created the same sense of criticism here. It's like the paparazzi is waiting at our door for something exciting to happen."

"Okay, you're right," Nellie agrees. "Remember when Cynthia's parents got a divorce? Everyone was in her face for months about it."

"Exactly. And everyone has divorced parents, so I don't know why it was such a huge deal. Imagine if I told everyone at that same time."

"I don't know, what about Devin? He could have helped you," she questions, as Devin was the only openly gay male at our school. Flamboyant and quite the dramatic, he checks a lot of the boxes of the stereotypical "gay" mold.

"He came out of the closet concomitantly as he came out of the womb, and we aren't exactly alike in any other ways," I retort. We were opposites in a lot of ways. I played sports in school; he performed in theater. He had style and was a pop culture enthusiast, while I wore my brother's hand-me-downs and only listened to country music. Speaking of, my brother also attended the same school and my coming out would have affected him too. It would have changed a lot. We all knew Devin for Devin, but people didn't know me as gay. Mentally, I threw myself back and forth into a wall trying to figure out how to transpire as me. "For some reason I couldn't wrap my mind around simply saying it out loud," I add. I tried to decide how to stop all the lies I told when anyone would ask, but ultimately I had no reason to as I couldn't imagine myself being with, well, anyone.

"Keith, I mean, we all questioned it but we just wanted to know. Not one of our friends would even imagine you were lying or being unauthentic; they would just think you were trapped." Nellie wraps her arm around me, going for a hug but promptly stopping and giving me a little shove instead. "How did you even manage being so happy all the time? You are always so positive and uplifting, yet hurting so hard on the inside without letting it show. Wow. That's so crazy you felt you had to do that! You know you can always come to me."

She stares at me critically for a moment, as if she's angry with me, but I know she isn't. "I am so happy to have you here and *so* happy to have you queer, baby!" Her arms wrap around my biceps restraining my ability to return the hug. Gaining composure, Nellie pulls back and begins jumping up and down with a screech while holding my shoulders to get a look at my red, teary-eyed face. "Keith, this is exciting! We can talk about boys! Who else knows? Am I the first person you told?"

At this point, I could sense Nellie's tumultuous side putting on her makeup for an appearance. I keep my head facing down but my eyes veer up in Nellie's direction, almost trying to hide from her. "I told Lily and Blair this weekend while we were all in the restroom at the fraternity party." She gives me a look of feigned offense, so I explain, "We were all drunk and I smiled at my phone like an idiot while we were crammed in a small ass bathroom. They basically read the texts over my shoulder, but they were going to find out sooner or later, and I'm glad it was while I had some liquid courage."

"I guess that's fair. Is there anyone else? Might as well have published it in the damn paper and told the Queen at this point," Nellie replies dramatically. I suspect the climax of her dramatics has yet to come.

"I told Scarlet before I told Lily and Blair." Nellie's mouth drops in shock. Scarlet works with us, but to be fair, I had known her years before I'd even met Nellie, so it didn't seem weird she was the first to know. I could keep this information to myself, but I figure why keep anymore secrets at this point?

"How did Scarlet get into this party? She doesn't even go to school with us. And how did that even come about before telling me?" As Nellie questions me, her tilted head reminds me of an angry dog. I can practically feel the sass radiating off her.

"Scarlet did not attend the party," I laugh. "I told her back in September when I had an incident with a boy of the past."

"Wait a minute, five months ago? And there were other boys? Of all people, you told Scarlet?" Nellie's voice begins to rise. "She has the biggest mouth of everyone here! How the hell hasn't anyone found out yet?"

"Pull up a chair," I say figuratively. "I'll tell you all about it."

"This should be good," Nellie responds, getting comfortable by leaning against the counter.

* * *

For about a year in high school, I talked to this boy from Virginia whom I also met through Instagram—a fine piece of work, with dark hair, dark eyes, around six foot two, and a beautiful thick accent. And ass, let's be real. He played basketball so he had a nice athletic build. We would spend hours on the phone just talking about our day, our home life, our upbringing—all of it.

If I needed support or grew lonely, he would be the one I would talk to. He had such a pure heart, gave good advice, and simply listened in times of need, as I did for him. We became our most vulnerable selves, together. We had this weird connection where we could be transparent around each other and had an understanding no one else could relate to. I began to think our only connection laid there, enduring loneliness in the closet, when he ghosted me for a while.

On a lonely night, I didn't know who else to reach out to, so I texted him to check in. His energy matched mine and we began sorrowfully chatting. Turns out he had been outed at one of his basketball games, which wreaked havoc in his little town. I imagine this is where his trust issues began, later leading him to always act hot or cold with no in-between. We drifted apart once more, but I would still receive random texts accusing me of telling someone at his school about our conversations.

One day, I gave in to what he wanted, arguing back. I made the points of, "Why would I when I'm going through the same thing?" or "I don't even know anyone in Virginia."

He didn't see the logic and threatened to out me "like I did to him." This conversation was all happening while I worked at Papa Smurf's and Scarlet worked the front of the store. I couldn't let her see me get upset, but I knew my emotions were going to boil over in short order. The next thing I knew, I was in the tiny bathroom in the back.

Sitting on the floor, I leaned my back to the wall, pulled my knees to my chest, and just let it all out. Never had I cried so much. Scarlet heard the sniffles and came in genuinely concerned. She knelt down and reached around me for a hug, holding me while I sobbed. Once I was calm enough to speak, I told her everything.

Scarlet grabbed my arms, encouragingly. "Keith, look at me. I love you so much and so does everyone else. Who cares if you're gay? He can literally fuck right off." I began laughing, smiling, hugging, and crying harder than I had before. Through the door to the bathroom, we were able to make out the song playing over the store speaker, "Let Me Be Myself" by 3 Doors Down. "Well, if destiny isn't telling us something!" she shouted, pulling me to my feet.

* * *

"Oh shit. Did I just gain a little respect for her? I don't want to, but damn." We share a laugh, turning my sappy ass mood around.

"She definitely made me realize your darkest secrets are what hurt you the most. I hadn't given any guy my attention since then, simply because I didn't trust them or myself, until now," I explain.

Nellie nods her head as hard as a sea lion at the zoo. "Ain't that the truth? Those secrets will absolutely haunt you. But you haven't told me much about @tarted3! Did you meet through Instagram?" She quickly changes the subject. "We don't fancy Virginia boy; he can kiss my ass!"

I laugh, feeling my face warm as I dream of my new obsession. "Nellie," I pause and look at her with glossy eyes. "He's sweet and adorable. We talked for the longest time on Instagram after he followed me and liked all of my pictures. We outgrew Instagram and began constantly Facetiming. We talk for hours about deep shit—intellectual conversations. The cutest thing he does is ask me what he did to make me smile each day." I look at her with the biggest smirk. "Isn't that so unheard of? And we've been sleeping together on Facetime since we can't physically be together. I'm so damn smitten."

"A true gem, Keith! Have you met yet? When are you going to do that? Have you talked about religion? That's a scary one. If he's like your grandma, we have to kick him to the curb. We don't have time for no preacher."

"We have. He isn't religious—we dodged the holy water." Nellie grabs my arm and throws her head back while her dark braids follow. "Sleeping on the phone is cute and all, but I'm hoping to drive there this weekend," I respond mid-laugh.

"Where is he?"

"Central Ohio, just an hour and a half away." My excitement bleeds through into my tone.

"Don't you work this weekend?" she questions. I give her a look with a pleading smile which tells it all. "Keith? Wait, no! Fuck you and no," she retorts dramatically.,

"Nellie, *please* trade me shifts! I'll work Friday night for you, and you'll work Saturday morning for me!" I plead my case as I point to the schedule hanging up on the wall.

She rolls her eyes and huffs, "Keith! Damn you." I can tell she's pondering the thought as she looks to the paper on the wall. I hold my breath and give her the biggest puppy dog eyes I can muster.

"Please, Nellie. I'm begging."

"Fine! But you owe me. I'm rescheduling my damn nail appointment for this."

CH. 2

CHALLENGE ACCEPTED

———

Heading to central Ohio creates such a surreal feeling. "I finally get to meet @tarted3!" I holler through the empty space in my car.

My '97 Honda Civic, also known as Hauni, rides smoothly while loaded down with a duffel bag and a backpack. The aesthetics of this baby are rather deceiving. Although Hauni runs like a champ, he looks like an absolute chump. He's green with ample sunspots on all sides of the car dividing the paint; he sports a black replacement hood, musty yellow old headlights, and a light brown interior with obvious discoloration, but no tears, which seems miraculous. While Hauni doesn't look like much, I know he'll get me where I need to go safely without any worries.

Driving North on I-71, I strictly listen to Andy Grammer. He's my go-to when I need to clear my mind and keep myself from thinking negative thoughts. I've driven this route for other occasions in the past and it's usually a simple ride, filled with calming corn fields and long stretches of road. However, the state of Ohio has decided to completely reconstruct—what seems to be—the whole stretch of road I endure this evening.

Red taillights constantly blind my eyes and halt my progress, causing the drive to drag along slowly. With the constant slowing down, I decide to FaceTime @tarted3 to help pass the time while traffic comes to a standstill.

"Oh no, are you hitting some traffic?" he implores as soon as he answers my call. I turn the camera to my face as my phone sits in its holder on my dash. He can now easily see my slightly disgruntled look.

"Yes, but Maps puts me there at 9:02:16 p.m. on the dot," I reply.

"Okay, not bad. Incredibly specific, but not bad. When you get here I can show you around my dorm and campus, take it easy tonight, and just make the most of the time. Does that sound good?"

"We can do whatever you want; I'm just excited to meet you."

With a smile, @tarted3 responds, "Me too; how could I not be with how beautiful you are? Look at this red glimmer on you." I laugh lightly, unsure if it's the red lights getting brighter or my blushing.

Nonetheless, I shake my head. "I'll see you soon."

My nerves are through the roof from juggling the stress of the traffic, making sure I arrive on time, and meeting this sweet boy for the first time. I crank up the volume on Andy to keep my spirits up.

* * *

As I approach Ohio State University, the dark of night takes over. I shoot @tarted3 a text while at a stop light, giving him a warning. "I am about fifteen minutes away from the garage!"

"Walking over now to finally meet you (:," he rapidly responds.

My mind runs wild during the last few minutes of the drive, after waiting almost a month to meet for the first time. *What will his first impression be of me? Of my little car? What if we don't vibe? What if he catfished me? Did I catfish him? Agh—why am I thinking this way?*

After talking myself down from the anxiety ledge, Maps guides my next move: "Turn right in eight hundred feet."

Pulling onto campus, the lighting changes from the dark road, which my headlights could barely illuminate, to florescent, vivid, new campus roads that are as bright as can be. At first glance, I see freshly paved sidewalks next to the parking garage, while across the street sits the brand new indoor athletic complex. As I make my way into the slick concrete-covered garage, I find a spot to park near the front entrance between two bright yellow lines.

I get out of Hauni, stretch and yawn as loudly as possible, causing my shirt to lift above my belly button. In the same moment I hear, "Hey you!" shouted from somewhere on the road. I turn my head to see a silhouette walking in my direction, with the shining streetlights creating a silhouetted view of him. As the silhouette approaches, the lighting shifts, revealing the blue shirt from the Instagram post I've been parading around Cincinnati.

Oh, shit. That's Toby Art Edmonson—in the flesh. Embarrassingly adjusting my shirt, my smile starts raging without control. As his face appears in my sight, I see his pearly white smile, dark perfectly placed hair, bushy eyebrows, rounded toned shoulders, and beautiful cocoa brown eyes fixated on me.

"Wow. Look at you." Something comes over me, and I'm mesmerized. My mind draws a blank. I'm unable to form words. I begin to realize this is the handsome guy that came onto *me*, calls *me* every day, and invited *me* to spend the weekend with him.

Keith! Get your shit together. I berate myself silently. *You basically came out of the closet to your friends because of this guy you've never even met. Be yourself; you finally have the opportunity. He's the only person who really knows you for you.*

The royal blue shirt becomes more and more realistic the closer we get to each other. I eventually get the whole full-frontal view and see his faded-black mid-cut Adidas socks, black Adidas soccer shoes, and black five-inch seam shorts. I also notice a quirky shoulder slightly shrugged up against his ear.

Next thing I know, he's within arm's length after all this time of being 110 miles away. Panic ensues, even after the pep talk I gave myself. Do we hug? Shake hands? Kiss? No. Instead, I wave as a substitute. "Not a bad drive, right?" Toby inquires while he goes in for a hug. I twist my body 180 degrees while wrapping one arm around his shoulders.

Such a bad hug. Why did I do that?

"It wasn't bad a drive, aside from construction. I talked to Nellie and jammed out to Andy Grammer, of course." Skipping the opportunity to ask about his day, I just leave it there.

"Uh oh, where did you tell your friends you were going?" he questions.

"Well… I didn't have to lie. I told her about you."

"This is new!" His silky brown eyes widen in surprise. "Let's walk the campus to stretch your legs. We can come back to your car; my dorm isn't far." We head for the lights outside of the garage. "It's really good to meet you, Keith. Do I need to introduce myself?"

Laughing, I ask, "I did my fair share of stalking but, does reintroducing yourself include a better hug?"

Smiling in approval, he hits me with the challenge of, "If you play your cards right." My ass loves it and I want redemption—so, challenge accepted.

As we begin our walk, Toby explains we are heading to the central area of campus connecting the different college focuses and the student life areas. The campus gives a fresh and new vibe from recent renovations and additions. The old red brick buildings make it such an interesting campus, radiating so much warmth while including plenty of added greenery. A pond serves as the centerpiece of campus, surrounded by a hilly walkway. The fluorescent lamp posts illuminate the beauty and detail of every building.

Toby has expressed his excitement for his college experience many times during our phone conversations, while pointing out all extracurriculars he plans to join. At twenty-three years old, only two years older than me, his college experience came a little late. He had to work promptly out of high school to save up for college. While not much older than me, he seemed to have a lot more experience in life than I had up to this point. Needless to say, I could tell he wanted to show off his new home.

"Tell me about Nellie. What did you say to her? She's the first person you've told?" Toby digs for more details as we walk.

"Oh man, you want the whole story, don't you?"

"Yes, I can't believe you haven't told me. You don't stop talking, yet you leave this out?" He nudges me to let me know he's joking.

"So, Nellie is my best friend, as you know. She's the happy, uplifting, musicals-and-drama type. She posts on Instagram for everyone to have a 'super sparkly day' and I don't know where I'd be without the girl. We work together at Papa Smurf's, and she's the reason I'm even here this weekend." Laughing, I add, "I made her switch shifts so I didn't have to work tomorrow."

"You didn't even ask her?"

"No no, of course I asked." I go on to explain how the trade occurred while our hands swing millimeters from each other as we walk. I desperately want to reach for it, but I'm too scared someone will see.

CH. 3

PITCH BLACK

———

Of course, I go into every detail of this story. His only comment is, "Oh, so you like when I ask what I did to make you smile, every day?" His in-person flirting lines up perfectly with all the previous comments he's made over the phone.

I can play the game, too. "I do. It's genuine, sweet, and gives me time to reflect on the day as a whole. You haven't failed yet, but can you keep up the streak?" Toby walks my way, pulls me closer, and wraps his arms around my neck for a hug—it clicks this time. He stands on the top of my toes as my arms wrap perfectly around his waist. We pull apart while my teeth gleam in the light.

As we continue our tour, we pass the education building. Here, Toby points to the brick structure with three tall, separated, rounded windows, explaining, "This will be the building where I'll be doing all my classes in a couple semesters."

"For your education degree? Three years to go, right?"

"Yeah, I'm in my second semester. I had to take a couple years off after graduating high school because I wasn't able to get funding. My family wouldn't sign any of the papers for me to get any loans. I had to wait until I could manage on my own. It's okay though; I'm here now and one step closer to having my own classroom."

"I've always wanted to have a classroom, mostly just to decorate it," I reply. We both laugh and begin to circle the lake, making our way to the bridge.

"Well you can come decorate mine because it will be bare if you don't." My mouth drops. "I'm kidding, I will spice it up somehow. I'm excited to be a teacher kids can look up to and confide in. So many teachers were someone to look up to for me, and it empowered me so much to just be different from my family."

"What did your family do to hurt—"

Ironically enough, his phone starts ringing, and the screen displays "Auntie Amanda" calling. He tilts his head as the reflection of the overhead campus lights glare in his gorgeous eyes. He asks kindly, "Do you mind if I answer this? It's my Auntie Amanda," as if I didn't see the bright screen. Of course, I grant permission. He doesn't move an inch, which allows me to overhear the conversation as we stand in the middle of the bridge over the lake. Toby gets a serious look on his face and begins to blink pretty heavily while looking into the distance.

"Rory shouldn't have gotten eighteen pets. I can't constantly dish out money, Aunt Amanda. It's beginning to affect me. Between him and our mother, it's just too much. I am in school; I can't work full time to support my unwilling family." He pauses and I can hear Auntie Amanda's voice fluctuate, bothered she's in the middle of this, shifting from stern to unconcerned with each word Toby says. "I have to check my bank account. I'll let you know what I can do." He hangs up the phone and turns to look at me. "I'm sorry, it could have been more important. I worry about her even though she's always bothered by Rory and me." His tone softens.

"No need to apologize. Are you okay? Seemed like she needed something." My elbows lay on the wooden railing, looking over the water. I hesitate and awkwardly reach out to squeeze his shoulder in comfort.

"I guess this would be a prime example of what you were asking about before she called." He takes a deep breath and turns to me. "You can't turn around and go home after I tell you, okay?"

As if I would, I think to myself. I just nod to him.

"My brother Rory and I are twins. Our mom technically raised us, but when I say raised, I mean she held legal guardianship. Auntie Amanda came to the rescue for us anytime we needed something, from picking us up at school when mom didn't to taking us to the doctor—it was always Aunt Amanda. Hell, mom even forgot us at the grocery store once and wouldn't pick up the phone when we had the clerk call her so Aunt Amanda came."

"Wow, I'm sorry. That must have been rough. How did she leave you at the store? It's rather difficult to forget two kids."

Toby looks up at me from staring at the water. He cracked a slight smile through the exhausted, stern look on his face and simply replies, "Drugs." My heart sinks to the bottom of the lake at this moment. My hand naturally reaches his back and I begin to rub it as we sit in silence.

"We obviously don't have the best relationship, but I try to keep the peace. My brother followed the same path for a while and collected all these animals along the way. I kid you not he has eighteen animals—reptiles, dogs, whatever they are—all in this one-bedroom house. Which is what Aunt Amanda just called about. His dog needs to go to the vet and he doesn't have the money to take it. He never musters the courage to call me directly. Mom will do the same thing when she's in a bind."

"Man, I know the stress drugs impose. My brother holds our family together for that same reason; I wouldn't want that roll. It would be great to keep the family around but at some point you have to draw the line, you know? You can't enable that lifestyle."

"I know. I'm not around them as often anymore so things are better relationship wise, but I still get the calls and they both still struggle. I don't want the blame on me for sending them into a spiral. Also, I will need somewhere to live this summer when I have to move from the dorms and my tentative plan is to stay at Aunt Amanda's."

"Fair. Do you think you would like living there? From what I heard, she doesn't seem the most welcoming," I ask hesitantly.

Letting out a deep sigh, "The thought of going there stresses me out. I'm not sure where else I would go though. Mom's will be out of the question when she finds out about me."

"What do you mean? Finds out you're gay?"

"Yes," he goes on, "the most disappointment I've ever felt in my mother, even with the drugs, had to have been when she made Rory move into his boyfriend's house after coming out to her. Rory hardly knew this boy and had basically just reached the age of consent. No mother in their right mind should put their kid in any situation of the sort. I'm sure Rory has already told her, so she is just waiting on me to call and ask so she can reject me."

"I assume you were inadvertently hurt, too?"

"Yeah—but to no surprise. I knew her capabilities existed to make the decision. She just confirmed it for me. I realized I should prepare to have the ability to make it on my own before most kids should have to."

This moment makes clear how hard it can be for every soul navigating coming out in a broken family. As we sit along the rail looking out at the moon, I take in those feelings while realizing how good I have it. The conversation makes me swoon more for Toby than before. Smiling at myself in the water, I realize I like him. I really do. His experiences are driving his purity; where he came from truly made up every part of who he has become.

In such a short time, I feel like I've known him forever.

Everything just falls into place on the bridge. I grab his waist and pull him over. He stands on his tippy toes, wraps his hands around my neck, then lays his head between my chin and my shoulder. My arms are around his waist, grabbing each side with the opposite hand. It's the most perfect hug again, more or less adding the last piece to a puzzle. I mean, redemption *is* sweet. I close my eyes to take in the feeling and when I open them, the lake shines so bright, with fluorescent reflections from all the overhead bulbs. "Let's call this our first hug," Toby jokes.

I sigh with overwhelming relief. "For sure our first." We release and head for the dorms. He grabs my finger and holds it as if it's my whole hand. Not how I imagined going about it earlier, but it leaves an impression that I grow to adore. "Do you think the people who give bad hugs think someone else giving bad hugs actually gives a good hug? Meaning two bad hugs are compatible to making one good hug?"

Toby looks at me and laughs. "Are these the things that go through your head?"

"Toby, don't even! It's a serious question here."

After retrieving my bags, we enter the lobby of the dorm and quickly turn into an elevator hall. I grab my bag from his hands as he shuffles for his keys. The arrow above the gray elevator door brightens as Toby presses the up button. I observe the white walls ahead where the corners meet above the green-and-yellow-striped caddy-cornered chair, sitting next to an oddly large, faux snake plant. While we wait, Toby lightly grabs my shoulders and turns me to face him. My excitement turns into anxiety when I see his shoulder go up in nervous tick position and his eyes batting.

"So I told you about my roommate Paul, yes?"

"Yeah, your roommate. He's here?"

"Yes, but he doesn't exactly know you're coming." He looks down and back up with a hope of preconceived forgiveness in his eyes. "I haven't come out to him, yet. I didn't plan on him being here this weekend. He told me he needed to go home so I assumed I had more time to prepare for the 'this boy I like is coming over' conversation. But, don't worry, you can sleep in my bed, I'll sleep on the floor tonight. If you're comfortable, we can cuddle tomorrow night and make the best of it."

I find myself focusing on the green stripe of the chair in the distance. "Oh, no worries. I get it; don't worry about it. He won't know I'm here." Internally, I'm disappointed. I've dreamed of holding this man through the night for the last few weeks. The opportunity is so close, yet so far.

Thanks, Paul.

Toby continues, relieved. "Okay, good. I didn't want you to be angry with me," he admits. Toby seems worrisome; small details get to him a lot. "Paul is pretty conservative in the way he grew up and we haven't had any gay talks come up, so I'm not sure how he would take it. I know I should have warned you earlier, but I really wanted you to come and I'm happy you're here."

"Me too. But I understand more than anyone. You have to tell everyone at your own pace." I smile at him and quickly get serious, "Thank you for sharing your family story. I know it isn't easy."

"Of course! You'll need to know where I came from to understand who I am going forward, if we keep this up." He laughs while we board the elevator. "I had a good time tonight. And you're just as gorgeous as I had imagined. You're a fun time and easy to talk to." I smile and reach for his finger. "With a perfect smile," Toby adds. He shyly looks down and reveals his perfect smile.

Incredibly in awe, he grabs my waist and lays his head on my chest, rubbing back and forth to get situated in the most perfect spot. I caress him around his waist. We don't say anything else; Toby just runs his fingers across the wood panels on the elevator wall and makes a knocking sound as each finger transitions to a new panel.

The elevator stops. While exiting, he carries my bag to room 317—such a gentleman. "Paul will probably be sleeping so let's try to keep quiet." Respectfully, I'm light on my feet for the next fifteen minutes as we proceed. He opens the door to a tiny corridor, which contains two light-colored wood doors. One leads to a restroom containing just a shower and a toilet, while the sink sits in the corridor between the two doors in an alcove. The gleaming fluorescent lights brighten the whole space. Across from the sink sits the mini fridge and microwave and the door to the bedroom and common space sit directly in line with the front door.

We manage to quietly get ready for bed.

"Are you good?" Toby whispers. The fluorescence highlights my nod. He grabs my finger again, shutting off the lights. I sense him come to a halt in front of me.

It's pitch black, so I don't move. His hands come around me again and up my stomach to my chest. Soon he reaches my shoulders and my chin. My vision never adjusts to the darkness so I just close my eyes and focus on his soft touch. I begin to get riled up and I adjust myself, pressing my body against his. His toes are on mine and the pressure from him elevating himself starts to sink into my feet. My heart races as I begin to get an enhanced Listerine smell from his mouth. The smell takes over and I release all the tension in my body.

My lips aren't prepared to meet another pair, but once they do, nothing else seems to matter. Toby lays one on me and *my god, it's magical*! His lips are mighty and full; they fit mine to perfection. I cup my hand around the back of his neck and into his hair.

Maybe the magic lies in the weeks' worth of sexual tension? Regardless, every touch feels so safe and so unerring. At this moment, all I know is I don't want to stop.

So we don't.

CH. 4

BEE

After my night alone in Toby's bed, Paul and Toby both have to work. I hear them attempting to quiet down while getting ready, but I act unbothered, faking sleep. I hear the front door of 317 open and close, which brings a small moment of peace and quiet. The door opens again, but I stay facing the wall.

Toby grabs my shoulder gently and pulls me over. "Good morning! I'm off to the library for my shift. If you want to come do some studying, you can. I'll get you a good spot by my desk. There's a towel on the bathroom sink and you can use my Irish Springs shampoo and body wash in the shower." I give him a nod as he leans in and gives me a kiss on the forehead. "I hate leaving you here."

I smile and roll over enough to pull his chin closer to kiss those lips before he heads off. He backs away, heading for the door again. I manage to say "thank you," barely able to form words with my scratchy morning voice.

"I'll see you soon, Keith. Get some more sleep." The door shuts for good this time. I lay there, basking in my giddiness instead of sleeping more.

I could get used to this.

* * *

Toby returns to room 317 to find me in the same place he left me, just readjusted with my back against the wall and a computer in my lap. He struts in with one hand behind his back while insulting me, "You haven't moved an inch, have you? I'm out here working all day and you're just lying in bed. This is what I have to look forward to in the years to come, huh?"

I laugh, "Boy, I've done my due diligence for the week. I'm done and I made sure of it." Ungracefully, I get out of bed and walk over to Toby, continuing "all to ensure I could be here with you." He lands a kiss on my lips and swoops his arm from behind his back.

I inspect the small, blue, rectangular package and I see the four, large colorful circles on it. He definitely brought my favorite candy. "I remembered you basically telling me you were a freak for only liking the Giant Chewy SweeTARTS. When I saw them, I just couldn't resist."

"I am not a freak. They're better and chewier," I say as I quickly throw the package on the ground to break the giants into smaller pieces.

Toby watches me in shock. "What's the point of them being *giant* if you're going to make them the size of the original?"

I open the blue package to find the four giant tarts, smashed like pieces of glass. "They hold the same consistency as they did when they were giant and the same delightful taste, just easier to eat now and still better than all the other types of SweeTARTS." He still looks confused. "You may never understand everything about me and I don't mind, as long as you support my strange habits."

"Well, when I take you to your next surprise, can you promise you won't tear it to pieces?"

He does ask nicely, but I can't be sure. "Tell me this surprise and I will decide."

"I figured we would go on an actual date. I did enjoy our FaceTime dates quite a bit," Toby grabs my hands, "but let's go out. We can finally sit across from one another and have a normal conversation."

"I like the sound of that, but don't say you made a fancy reservation." My eyes grew small upon my cheeks rising with a simper. "Only because I didn't bring clothes for fancy places and also, I'd rather get six margaritas before I spend sixty dollars on shrimp tartare."

"My kind of guy," he assures me, "don't worry, we can wear anything. But, I do recall you telling me you enjoy sushi." Nodding, I continue to listen. "You also told me they never have what you want so you basically tell them to take most items off and substitute them."

Toby bounces around the room to begin getting ready while I reply, "I did mention it, yeah."

"So this place allows you to make your own sushi roll. It's their niche! I have been once before with Brock."

The grin on my face becomes hard to hide once I realize he had taken notes. "Oh, wait, I'm excited. That sounds great! Tell me more about Brock. I've heard you talk about him but I don't know a lot."

"Brock has become one of my good friends. He, Kevin, Annie, and I hang out quite a bit."

"What do you mean by, *become*?"

"When we first met, we were straight friends who hooked up. We basically used each other to experiment with our sexuality and didn't really talk much about it, to anyone. We dissolved the situation pretty quickly once we saw each other around more often and developed the same friend group here."

"So, has he come out to everyone now or still experimenting?"

"I'm not sure, actually. As I said, we kind of just never talk about it. He and Kevin were the same way so he obviously knows. Annie should know but she might just be oblivious to us all being gay. She's just too pure." Toby laughs at his thoughts of Annie.

"I would be intrigued to see the dynamic of the four of you," I chuckle at the thought. "As long as I don't have anything to worry about with Brock, I'm okay." I smirk and walk over to Toby rummaging in the closet.

Turning around to give me a kiss, he reassures me, "Trust me, you definitely have nothing to worry about."

* * *

Pleasantly surprised, we pull up to this old garage shop refurbished into an all-black sushi empire. Two garage doors sit above heads while the air flows in. The inside has a minimalist white design with a pop of bright green color in the centerpieces and art on the wall, which makes it work despite being a garage.

Before I can get out of the car, Toby runs around to open my door. What a sweetie! He looks around before giving me a kiss. Inside, the host cheerily seats us at a table decorated with a single rose in a tall vase while a bottle of wine joins the table as we sit.

"Did you ask them to do this?" I question while looking at the beauty of the table. It seems a little over the top for Toby's taste.

He laughs and explains, "Here's the thing. I told them tonight would be our first real date and explained the situation. They originally weren't able to fit us in but the girl at the front took down my number to see what she could do. She ended up calling me back when someone canceled. It worked out really well. But, no, I did not ask them for the candles or the rose"—the nervous tick begins again—"just the wine."

"Baby, it's great. They really have gone the extra mile for you. They didn't have to do all of this for us. I do love a good surprise, though. They deserve a nice tip when we are finished!"

"Yeah, for sure a good tip. I didn't want you to see me as an overachiever, but we have yet to formally go out so I wanted to put in a little more effort after we met yesterday."

"Can I be honest?" I ask as I pour the wine in the glasses provided on the table.

"Only if it's positive honesty. Your tone makes me scared you're about to get in the car and go back to Cincinnati."

Laughing, "I didn't mean to sound negative. What I intended to say is about the kiss in your foyer."

"What about it, *baby*?" He adds emphasis, making fun of me.

"Ahh, I just wanted to tell you my taste buds were almost as satisfied as they were when I ate the candy you brought me." I look up at him with a soft smile while focusing on grabbing the stem of my glass.

"Oh man, I need to step up my kissing game?" he laughs while leaning on the back of his chair. "Well, I definitely realized I'd been slacking once we kissed."

"Are you being serious?" I genuinely can't tell. "I really don't think you have been so far. We've only texted and talked on the phone every day for the last three weeks," I laugh. "There's only so much you can do."

He leans in my direction, placing his chest on the edge of the table while grabbing my leg underneath— my heart flutters. "I. Want. To. Do. More." He whispers, "Will you allow it?"

I copy his lean, replying, "Of course. I wish you could make up for that kiss right now." I look back and forth from his right eye to his left.

"I never want to stop. I do want to take things slow with you, though." He nervously looks down. "I want our first time to feel like nothing in the world matters. Like it's me and you."

"I'm okay with taking it slow. I want more from you than just your penis, Toby."

He stands up while laughing at my directness, "At least I tried to be cute! I have to use the restroom." As he walks past me, he leans over and kisses my head. The butterflies fly rampant in my stomach. I've never experienced this kind of treatment in public. It's extremely new to me so I can't really tell if these feelings are about the boy or the PDA—hopefully the boy.

* * *

Our sushi comes out, just how I want for the first time in history, with cream cheese, shrimp, avocado, panko, spicy mayonnaise, and roe. We share a plate of edamame and down the bottle of wine while cleaning every plate. We take in the chatter of everyone around us and lean back, brim as can be.

I interrupt the chatter with a serious tone, "Does a relationship scare you?"

"Oh gosh, going deep before I can even digest my food, aren't you?" I let out a small laugh. He continues, "It's terrifying. I don't know how a relationship works. I don't even know who I am, yet."

I make a "me too" gesture by pointing at my chest and holding up two fingers.

"Yesterday and today, I have been able to explore *myself* more than ever before. Getting my family to accept my male partner might be what scares me the most. I don't want to lose anyone and maybe my biggest fear is simply rejection, not being gay."

"Which makes complete sense. The people around you are important; they've helped mold you into who you are, partially creating the issue—I'm in the same boat."

"Yeah, they're a big part of why I'm afraid of being gay." We chuckle because we know the truth this holds. "They've instilled their heteronormative standards and beliefs in me," Toby continues.

I chime in, "Yeah, not to mention the negativity associated with the gay community, which we inadvertently inherited while growing up also interferes with coming out and being our true selves."

Toby nods, "It's just tricky 'cause they don't mean to make it this way. Society has just evolved into this. Now we face the big task at hand—reversing it."

"My mom would definitely be on board; we just don't talk about deep topics often."

"From what you told me, it seems as if she would be. My mom, on the other hand, made it clear when she kicked Rory out she would not be reversing any of those beliefs if we were gay. She created us and she hates us for who we are." He laughed at himself for a second, then looked up at me. "I've accepted it. She will have to fix her own issues before I can even think twice about taking her opinion into consideration."

"Only time can tell, baby." I reached under the table for his thigh. "She will realize what she continues to push away one of these days—Rory, too. I'm sure he's great."

"He's a nut, but he's doing good and trying to better himself every day. He's a good brother; he just has had a lot of pressure on him from a young age."

"I feel you have had the same pressure. You were just able to foresee it coming and cope with it before it happened. He didn't have that luxury, but you can make the best out of your situation, since you know what's to come."

"He definitely did not, which is rather unfortunate." As he said this, I notice a slight buzzing. I turn my head in all directions, asking, "What are you doing?"

Smiling at each other, I say, "Do you not hear the buzzing?"

"Oh, I do now." Next thing you know there's a bee on my wasabi. "Look at the little guy. He flew in from the garage."

I lean in to get a closer look. "You won't find anything that spicy out in the big world—*bee* careful!" I quickly realize Toby has never heard my pet voice before. My eyes widen and I look at him. Keeping my act up, I continue, "What? There's a *bee* on my wasa-*bee, beebee!*"

He laughs endlessly and the bee sticks around until Toby slaps his hand on the table trying to pull himself together. "Bye little beebee!" He says to the bee. "I'm gonna start calling you beebee. My little bee. It's better than *baby.*"

"I agree, pet names are the scariest thing about a relationship," I laugh at our irrational fear.

As we exit the restaurant and walk to the car, he grabs my hand—well, my finger—until he opens the passenger door.

He leans on the door watching me and I kiss his cheek with a thank you.

The bee is definitely scarier than PDA. Little do I know what scary actually looks like.

CH. 5

DAMN EXAM

———

"I am just not into this today. What demon possessed me to take all my classes on Mondays and Wednesdays?" Blair says, walking through the University of Cincinnati's student center.

Lily puts her in her place quickly. "You said you wanted to stay home with your damn cats the rest of the week, so you chose this." The three of us share an obnoxious laugh as we walk into the cafeteria area.

"Uh, how dare you? Thanks for the reminder. I can now vividly see my little tabby at home alone," Blair realizes while brushing her hand through her straight, black hair. She notices the faces of the rest of her audience. "Wow, everyone has finally realized they signed up for hell here. I do not see one smile in this establishment."

"I know; someone pissed in everyone's Cheerios this morning, didn't they?" I decide to chime in.

"Stop. Not the Cheerios! Does anyone even eat those anymore?" Lily replies in her usual happy and humorous way. This is the same way she joked when we awkwardly met standing in the orientation line as freshmen. She popped a joke about how the lady directing everyone sounded similar to the HR slug lady in *Monsters Inc.* "Doesn't matter, I guess. Keith, you're rather happy today. Which calls for—"

They minimize the gap between their shoulders as they sing in unison, "A story of the week!"

My cheeks turn red with the biggest grin. "What possesses you to cause a scene everywhere we go?"

"Well, good sir, we care about you and your recent development in your—" she looks around and whispers the one word, "*queer,* life. So, if you will, start talking."

As we join the line to grab our food I reply, "Let's wait 'til we are at the table to discuss this topic. What did you all do this weekend?"

"Oh you know, same old shit, different weekend. Though, we didn't hang around your fraternity for once. We just tried out a different one where we did the same shit we would do with yours." We make it to a table just as Blair finishes talking about how a Franzia wine bag busted open while mid-pour, arms fully extended, with the wine flowing into her mouth and not a glass. "Yeah, it made a mess. Actually, I'm the mess. Luckily, I was dressed in all black to match my Gemini aesthetic."

Blair and I met in a similar situation; just substitute the wine for beer and add a hoppy stench and you end up with the beautiful friendship we have now.

"Well, this just sounds like the most Alpha Omega time! I'm sad I missed all the fun." They sense my inauthenticity.

"No you're not! Tell us about this boy. We have been patient long enough," Blair demands.

"Okay, fair." I don't know where to begin, but somehow, over the next hour, I tell them everything possible.

Throughout the story, they shower me with huge grins and positive remarks. Lily claps her long hands, constantly saying "I love this so much" with an abrupt squeal of excitement.

* * *

Post our dreaded day of classes, I meet up again with Blair and Lily at the library where we routinely study. Langsam Library's brown concrete structure remained in its original state while the inside underwent plenty of renovations. You would never expect the outside dungeon vibe to house a bright, happy place. No one thoroughly enjoyed studying there, but the renovations make it bearable.

We typically pop up to the second level in the back corner, where tables are tucked away in a little corridor surrounded by three walls. It's usually a battle to find a spot anywhere else, but my fraternity has someone there constantly so we can rotate through.

My two favorite brothers, Nolan and Alex, chat about business school nonsense.

"Oh yeah, the worst!" I obnoxiously joke to interrupt them, while the three of us walk to the head of the table, taking the two available seats and pulling up a third.

"What's going on guys? What will we be working on?" Nolan inquires.

Blair responds, "Nolan, you know this always becomes more of a social hour than study time. My books will be open and so will my mouth."

"Blair! We have an exam Wednesday; we have content to actually learn. Do you know what that means?" Alex stresses more often than not in the library, mostly from slacking when he isn't there.

"Sweetie, you have over twenty-four hours. I have aced a biology final with less studying time and I am a marketing major. You all will do great." Alex rolls his eyes at Blair's carelessness. We continue to shoot the shit and laugh for a bit, but finally shift our focus to studying for our respective exams.

Eventually, Alex jumps up to walk a lap around the library to clear his mind and take a break from studying, something we do often. Nolan and I begin to take a little break, too. "How did the party go this weekend?" I ask.

"Buddy, we had a ball. Of course, too many drinks. The new guys were there and they were just having a great time. It reminded me of when we were new members."

"Yeah, we had the best time. We would just hang out and ask about how we all grew up and genuinely were so excited to get to know everyone. We acted as if every person we met would be our best friend forever. You're literally the only friend I hang out with regularly now."

"I don't know where I'd be without you, buddy!" Nolan absolutely has the sweetest, most sincere heart. "Where were you this weekend? I meant to text you."

Lily overhears, tucks her thin, dirty blonde hair behind her ear, and chimes in, "Yeah! where were you this weekend, Keith?"

My legs cross under the table and I can feel an angst come over my body. "Out of town."

"Nice. Where did you go?" Nolan unknowingly pries.

"Columbus, visiting some friends. I had a good time." I attempt to dull down the topic so he doesn't ask any more questions.

Lily gives me a wide-eyed look with her green beauties, which Nolan sees. "What was that look? Why did you give him a look?" He questions Lily, who still pointedly looks at me.

My face gets red and I begin rubbing my hands together, looking down at the white, speckled table. Blair jumps in at this point. "Keith, isn't he one of your best friends?"

"I mean, yeah." I reply.

"What are you all talking about?" Nolan nearly gets frustrated. "Do you all need to fill me in on something?"

"I visited someone I've been talking to."

"Really? Who is she?" he asks.

And here it goes again.

I know he will love me no matter what, but the fear continually haunts my brain. I begin shaking and Nolan notices. The middle of his eyebrows pull down, almost meeting his nose in a look of worry. Finally, I grab my phone, open up my Instagram account, and pull up a photo of my gorgeous, brown-eyed boy. I stare at it for a while before bringing the phone down to my chest, hiding the screen. "Promise this won't change anything?"

"What could possibly change anything, buddy? Of course, I promise." I turn the phone over to Nolan. "Oh shit." His eyes widen and he looks up at me, over at the girls, then back at me. "He's a guy. You're gay?" My hand starts shaking and the water begins filling my eyes. A couple tears drop on the speckled table. "Dude, that's awesome! Why are you crying? He's a good-looking dude. Why didn't you tell me? I've always wanted a gay best friend." He looks to Lily and Blair, who nod in agreement.

"It isn't simple, Nolan. It's always been perceived so negatively," I sniffle between my words.

Nolan stands up and gives me a hug. "Man, you know I would take a bullet for you no matter what." As he sits back down, he gets serious. "You are my best friend, like Blair said. I could care less who you're out there railing. As long as you're happy and continue being your amazing self, who gives a shit?"

"Yeah, I'm beginning to realize this myself. Sorry, I didn't mean to get emotional. Hiding something for so long just creates false scenarios in your head for when you do tell someone, you know?"

"Well, buddy, maybe I don't know to this extent. But, I'm glad you can be up front about it now. How long have you been liking dudes?"

"A long time. I don't know, forever? It's hard to pinpoint a time. The norm has always been being straight, so I forced myself into heterosexual relationships and kind of halted my exploration into myself."

"Well, now is your time to shine. This has been eating at you for quite some time, hasn't it?"

"Yeah, people don't realize how long their words and actions stick with someone. The world can be cruel without even knowing the effect they have on someone in the long haul."

"Shit. They can't hurt you anymore, buddy. Go out there and be who you are. You have people who love you. I'm so glad you told me!"

"Yeah, baby boy, be who you are!" Lily jumps in with a huge smile, per usual.

"Thank you all. You all are truly the best." I pause for a moment, wiping the last little tear from my eye. "Isn't there a rule against being this emotional on a Monday?" As the words come out of my mouth, I look over to see Alex turn the corner.

He takes note of everyone's focus on me and does the same. "Why are we so emotional?"

With a laugh I say, "This damn exam gives me the worst anxiety."

"You should be thrilled you missed it. His breathing grew slightly heavier than a damn French bulldog." Blair jokes.

Lily laughs while adding, "The snot seemed similar, too." We all join in on the laughter.

At this moment, I realize I can do this at my own pace, well, in theory.

CH. 6

DEEPEST FEAR

Upon a fashionably late arrival to Saturday's tailgate, Nolan tosses over a beer to Nellie and me. "Catch up!" he yells.

"Oh gosh, how many beers deep are you boys? What time did you get here to start the party?" Nellie wonders aloud.

"Well, Nellie, as the tailgate chairs in our fraternity, Nolan and I have been preparing for the last football game for a while. We have corn hole and beer pong, plenty of beer, and we were able to rent a huge speaker for the back of my truck," Alex replies.

Nolan ignores Alex's bragging. "We've both had about five." Of course he kept track. He has the brains and Alex has the ideas, which makes them a great team.

"We've got a few hours until the game, you guys. Are you going to make it?" I joke.

"Of course we are; we always do!" they reply. Nellie and I look at each other and laugh.

"I mean at the rivalry game, you both ended up asleep on that truck bed of yours." Nellie points to the blacked-out F-150.

"Not a bad place to sleep, am I right, Nolan?" Alex reaches out to get a fist bump, maybe for having a cool truck or maybe for being a nuisance. I can't really tell. Nolan denies the bump.

"What about homecoming, when you weren't allowed in for sneaking your beers in?" I couldn't let them forget how they almost got our whole group turned away.

Nolan responds rather slowly, "Well, we made it *to* the game, we just didn't get *in* the game." Fair point.

"Anyway, so many people will be here today! It should be a ton of fun; I'm glad you made it. Please, help yourselves to whatever you want. We probably got *way* too much." Moments like these are when Alex makes you forget about most of the idiotic things he does. He has a kind heart but wants everyone to befriend him so badly—hence the reason he bought an F-150.

Nellie and I are decked out in our red and black, as is everyone else, but we are a bit over the top—face paint, tattoos on our faces, and accessories galore. We run over to Lily and Blair once we notice them among the crowd. I can tell they are a few beers in as well from the roaring shrieks they let out when they see us walk their way.

"Look at you two; y'all are so *hot*! Let's shotgun a beer!" Blair never fails to get straight to the point. Contrary to past experiences, we have a successful shotgun moment. As time goes on, people begin to get louder, stumble more, and put one hell of a dent in the beers Alex brought.

Getting rather chatty myself, I start a conversation with one of the senior fraternity brothers. As we wrap up talking about fraternity business, he asks, "So, I heard you were seeing someone?"

Did he just make this up or did someone tell him I've been seeing someone? Maybe he has me confused with another brother.

After a brief pause, I casually respond, "No, just living my life here. I work full time and go to school full time; I don't have any more time to give. That's why I'm the secretary and not the president of the fraternity." He seems confused but laughs it off. "Are you seeing anyone?" After I ask, I realize I've made a mistake as he begins going on and on about a girl he's been dating. I zone out.

My thoughts veer to Toby, wondering if he texted me and if I should sneak away to call him. I realize I'm not looking up anymore and refocus on my fraternity brother, who seems to still be talking. I nod as if I'm paying attention but then he asks me, "How do I come back from that?" I don't know how to respond; I start to panic internally.

Oof, what am I supposed to say here? I don't know how to date.

Luckily, Lily comes just in time to save me from my thoughts, and frankly, this conversation. I instantly thank her as she drags me over to the truck. She pulls me up on the bed as it bounces from all the bodies dancing. The boys chose only the best songs, playing everything from Kesha to Bon Jovi.

Lily leans over, screaming in my ear, "Has this truck ever seen this much action?"

"Hell no, these shocks didn't know their purpose until this moment," I shout back.

Next thing I know, we're singing Taylor Swift's "Welcome to New York" at the top of our lungs. I look at Lily as Taylor Swift serenades us with a line about boys liking boys. Lily and I share—what we think is—a secretive grin. While feeling incredibly great, we then realize Eddie, another fraternity brother of mine, has grabbed my shoulders as he grins. He lets go quickly enough, but he's given me concern.

I yell over the music in Lily's ear, "Did he just grab my shoulders while it said the boys line?"

"He definitely did, but there's no way he knows, right?" she replies.

"You didn't tell anyone, did you?" I ask nervously.

"I would never—and Blair wouldn't either." We hop down from the truck and I stumble around the parking lot, losing Lily in the crowd while hunting down Nolan, the only other person who knows. I pull him aside from a conversation he's in the middle of, with no apology or warning. "You didn't tell anyone about our conversation in the library, did you?" I question.

"What? Buddy, are you kidding?" He gives my upper arm a drunken nudge. "I wouldn't dream of it. Why? What's going on?"

"Eddie just grabbed my shoulders during a Taylor Swift song when she sings about boys liking boys. Lily saw it too. It seemed extremely odd," I explain, scanning the crowd of folks attending the tailgate.

"Are you sure?" he asks skeptically.

"Yes, I'm not tanked. I know what he did."

"Who else knows?"

"You, Lily, Blair, and Nellie. But I know none of you would say anything."

"What if it was a coincidence? Let it go and have fun, dude. Besides, even if he did know, he clearly doesn't think any differently of you." We begin to walk away from the crowd.

"Maybe he doesn't, but what about everyone else? Eddie has more of an open mind than most guys here." I start to get mildly emotional at this point, as fear mixes with my slight buzz. "You have no idea how terrifying becoming the 'gay guy' can be. It just means after all these years of being called a 'fag' and 'queer,' they get the satisfaction of being right, as much as I tried to avoid it."

"Why don't you want them being right about you being gay? We love who you are. It isn't a bad thing, Keith."

We both stop as I explain to Nolan, "Being gay isn't a good thing to most people. People have called me those names for years and not once have they been used as a term of endearment." I laugh at myself to avoid getting emotional. Those words have the most negative, hateful connotation any words can carry, and I hid because people have used them to describe me for years. "Who knows how differently some of these guys will look at me, even if I am the same person."

"If anyone doesn't like who you are just because you're gay, then they don't have a damn place in your life as far as I'm concerned. And that's as far as you're concerned, too. I mean, face it Keith, we hardly hang out with any of these people anyway. We may be at the same function, but we only hang out with each other, Blair, Lily, and Nellie. This fraternity thing is hardly what it seemed when we signed up, man." I agree and nod my head, finally starting to calm down. I look into Nolan's perfect hazel eyes as he says, "Live your truth, buddy."

I take a deep breath, calling myself out. "Nolan, I just freaked out and I don't even know if anyone knows." We laugh again.

"Come on dude, let's get to this game." We rejoin the group.

However, it doesn't ease my anxiety when Nolan and I approach Alex and Nellie, who are with Eddie. I look at Nellie and sarcastically admonish her, "Where have you been, Nellie?"

"Me? I've been here, all around."

I giggle a bit, asking her, "How many drinks have you had?"

"Oh, I feel good. Don't worry about me." She smiles easily.

"Yeah, drink all you need. There. Is. Plenty. And, *we* need to go to the game soon," Alex says, drunkenly checking Nellie out.

Nellie scoffs, but he has a point. Nellie begins to ditch and I get the vibe, following after her. I can't help but immediately ask, "You didn't mention Toby to anyone, did you?"

She jerks her head up, dramatically puts her hand on her chest, and says, "Bitch, no. Why would I do that?"

"Well, it seems Eddie knows."

"You didn't tell him?" she asks.

"No, we never speak to each other, but it seemed he knew when we were dancing around on the truck earlier."

"Who else knows? Blair, Lily, Nolan, and Alex?" She seems so confident.

"Alex? I never told him."

"How does he know, then? He brought it up to me like it was in the *New York Times*."

"*Shit…* Nellie, how did he find out?"

"We need to find Lily, Blair, and Nolan." I head for the cooler to grab another beer and I chug it down. I do another scan to find my friends while Nellie stands on the cooler for a better angle. As I scan the crowd, I feel the stares. I can feel the news being spread one by one, all around me. Or maybe they are wondering why Nellie has made her way on top of the cooler. I'm not sure, but my anxiety doesn't let me believe for a second they are all worried about Nellie.

Then it dawns on me. I look up to see a line of brick buildings and the stadium in the far distance. Alex isn't dumb. I tug Nellie's arm, bringing her down from the cooler. "Alex overheard us at the library. He must have told Eddie."

"Eddie and Alex are still over there, but I can't find Blair or Lily." Nellie points at the corn hole boards on the opposite side of the parking lot.

I walk with purpose to the corn hole boards. Ignoring Alex, who greets me as I walk up, I begin interrogating Eddie. "Who told you?"

"Who told me what?" he replies. Alex walks up next to him, eyebrows raised and ears perked back.

"I may have told him," Alex admits while reaching for my shoulder.

Knocking his hand away, I turn to him. "I didn't even tell *you*. What makes *you* think it's okay to tell someone else? That is *not* your story to tell, Alex!" Nellie approaches with the gang all in tow at the perfect time. Nolan starts to pull me away, sensing my anger, but I resist enough to continue berating Alex. "How *dare you!*"

"I haven't told anyone else. It's okay, Keith. You're my brother no matter what," Eddie chimes in.

"It's not about you. That isn't the point. *He* doesn't get to have those moments for me. *He* doesn't determine when I'm comfortable telling someone." I start crying and begin falling to the ground. Nolan catches me before I make it to the concrete and begins walking away with me. I can hear Blair and Lily's voices berating Alex, but they fade as we walk further away. They are trying to get more information out of Alex's drunk ass. I rip away from Nolan, turn back, and project my voice through my tears. "It's okay, guys. I'm just going home," I tell them.

"You can't walk home alone. I'll go with you," Nellie offers while catching up to us. Nolan offers the same.

"Really! I can't handle being around people. Go to the game; I can call a ride if I need to." I just want to talk to Toby in private. He'll know what to say. He knows how to make me feel better. Reluctantly, Nolan and Nellie send me off with big hugs and 'I love you's.' As I begin to walk away, I realize I have never been this upset or rattled before. I have never berated someone *that* harshly before, nor have I ever snapped in such disarray. But I can't help but feel he deserved it.

Once I get to the main road it's a straight shot back to campus, so I mindlessly walk. I get out my phone to find four unread texts from Toby. I got so caught up in the whole Eddie and Alex thing I completely forgot we were texting. I see I've missed a couple.

"Hope you enjoy the game. Don't get too wasted, okay?"

"I just got off work. I miss you."

"But I hope you're having fun."

"You need a day with your pals!"

I press the call button, hoping he'll pick up while mumbling, "Please, please, please!" under my breath and looking up at the sky. I just need to hear his voice so I know everything will be okay.

The ringing stops, and a voice I know and love powers through, "Hi baby boy. How's the game?"

"Toby! I'm glad you answered." I take a deep breath. "I'm leaving the tailgate."

"You're headed to the game now?"

"No, I'm going home."

"Wait, why? Are you okay?"

I begin to sniffle and I can feel the tears attempt to bust out of my eyes again. "Yeah." I can barely speak.

"No you're not. What happened? Tell me. Are you okay, physically?"

"I'm okay, Toby. I just wish you were here."

"I would be if I could. You know I had to work this morning. I can be there in about two hours—I can head there now. What's going on?" I hear ruffling and a zipper zipping.

"No, you don't have to come. I'll be okay; everything happens for a reason. I just wanted to hear your voice. It comforts me for some reason."

"Oh yeah? I could comfort you more if I come there, *and* if I knew what happened."

"I always want to hold you. You really don't have to come, though. I'm almost home and I'm going to take a nap."

"Do you want to tell me what happened?"

"I will later. I don't want to talk about it now. I called so you could take my mind off it. I didn't mean to start crying like a little bitch." We share a small laugh and we don't talk about it. Instead, he goes on a monologue about work, how literature can be interpreted in so many ways, and how he can't wait to portray that message to his students when he has a classroom.

It's rather adorable, the excitement in his voice. He lets me forget about the day I had, and I just listen and walk. It's exactly what I need.

* * *

My phone vibrates on the bed, startling me from my nap. I take a deep breath and search for my phone as it begins vibrating for a second time. Toby's name lights up my screen.

"Hey, sorry. I took a nap."

"I'm sorry I woke you up, handsome. How do you feel?"

"I'm feeling that today has been an absolute nightmare." I reply dryly.

"What if I told you I had a surprise for you?"

I slowly rise, telling Toby, "I can't handle a surprise right now, bee."

"Maybe look over your balcony."

I make my way over to the door in my room connecting to the balcony. It's a shitty door so I struggle to open it as the bottom is stuck on the wood frame. "You're not outside, are you?"

"Well..." Toby stands in the street, leaning on his silver Corolla holding a pizza and a grocery bag. My emotions do a one-eighty. Hanging up the phone, I signal him over and meet him at the corridor doorway. I grab the pizza from him and tuck it away on the steps for now. I pull his hand toward me and wrap my arms perfectly around his waist. He places his hands around my neck, causing the bag to bounce off my back a couple times until it settles.

"What are you doing here?" I ask, pulling him closer to me.

"I couldn't let you be sad and alone." I pull my face back and look at him. I give him a gentle kiss. Then he descends from his tippy toes and we make our way up to my apartment. Luckily, my roommate, Drew, attended the football game and no more confronting has to ensue.

We munch on the pizza in bed, cuddle, and I tell him what happened at the tailgate. He holds me tight, lets me be vulnerable, and makes me feel like it doesn't even matter. After explaining every in and out of my day and the backstory of my talk with Nolan at the library, we end up talking into the wee hours of the morning.

Just before we decide to get some sleep he asks me, "Can I ask you one more thing?"

"Ask away, baby."

"Can you tell me your deepest fear? And I don't mean spiders or snakes—your brain may be wired in a weird way to make you scared of some non-tangible thing that really shouldn't actually be scary."

I ponder silently while Toby respects the time I need to process the question. "If you would have asked me this yesterday, I would have said, 'someone spreading my darkest secret.'"

He smirks and quietly responds, "Look at that, you lived through your biggest fear. Maybe there's nothing to really be afraid of after all!"

Deep in thought, I stare at the balcony door in my room. "I guess you're right." I settle into bed and turn to face Toby. I find his lips with my hand and lean in to give him one last kiss. "Sleep tight, bee."

We cuddle up, holding each other softly, face to face.

Just as my eyes roll back for a deep sleep, I hear, "Keith, are you awake?"

I let out a faint moan and softly say, "Yes, babe."

"Can I ask you something?"

"Of course."

He pulls me a little closer, kisses my forehead, and asks, "Can we make this official?"

"Make what official?"

"Us." My heart pounds in my chest. I squeeze him tighter as he asks, "Will you be my boyfriend?"

I push my head closer and kiss those sweet lips. "Most definitely, bee."

NEW GIRL

—

It's my third consecutive weekend in Columbus since Tailgate. I've drifted away from most of my friends in Cincinnati, simply to avoid the "are you okay" questioning.

Toby and I make a conscious effort to stay on campus to avoid spending money, as any college student tries to do. We study, play soccer on the new fields, and drink some beers in his dorm. Our days become monotonous.

Timing couldn't have been better. "Brock, Kevin, and Annie invited us to play a round of laser tag today. Would you want to meet them?" Toby asks.

Being around new people sounds perfect. "I want nothing more!"

"Good, because I already told them we are coming." We laugh. "I knew you wouldn't say no, but, yeah, I told them you were staying with me earlier in the week. They're excited to meet you."

"Well, I am just flattered," I say with some shock in my voice. "When do the festivities begin?"

"In about an hour and a half."

My eyes widen. "And you tell me this now?" He nods and I add on, "You better get in the shower. You stink!"

"Oh, it's like that?" He wraps his arms around me from behind.

"Ugh, it's rubbing off on me, bee. Make it stop!" He releases me after we fall on the bed. "Okay, go shower!" I smack his ass for a little encouragement, which seems to work.

I hang over the sink while brushing my teeth, as he opens the bathroom door and the smell of Irish Springs slaps me in the face. He walks up behind me in his towel while grabbing my waist. "You smell amazing. You look amazing. I just can't get enough," I feed his ego. He backs away before his towel almost falls off. He's still a little modest around me.

* * *

In the middle of a jam session in the car, we pull up to a rather ominous, red brick building with ample neon signage that screams arcade. Toby turns the radio volume down, looks to me, and says, "Bee, I have to tell you this now."

Oh great. What now?

He continues, "I haven't told them what's going on with us, yet."

I give him a look, which probably comes across as more of a "what the fuck?" But at this point in our relationship, it's weird he hasn't told them yet. "It hasn't come up in conversation and I haven't really come out to them—well, Annie, at least. I plan on mentioning it tonight, after they see how great you are," he quickly explains.

After being slapped with déjà vu, I tell him, "Well, it's your story to tell. If you feel tonight would be a good night, then just let me know how I can help. Who did you say I am, then?" I question.

"A friend. I didn't really specify."

Just a friend. Okay. "We can lay low. You make the moves, bee."

His head tilts as we park, turning toward me while he nervously blinks. "You're okay with that?"

"I mean, yeah, I don't really have a choice and I know this stuff takes time. Do what you have to do. Have you told them you're gay yet? I thought you were working on this."

"Kevin and Brock know as we've had our past. Annie may not; we haven't exactly had the conversation, but she knows about Kevin and Brock so she wouldn't care by any means." He takes a pause. "I'm not worried about them knowing. I just hadn't had the chance to bring us up yet."

"I get it. I really do. This needs to happen on your own terms." Oof, a blow to the gut. It's disappointing he doesn't seem to share the same excitement about us dating as I do. Hell, I told my friends I'm gay after two weeks of talking to him. Laughing off the pain, I reply, "I will offer you a piece of advice: just bring it up."

He gives me a defeated look and says, "Yeah, you're right."

At this point, I don't want to say the wrong thing, but curiosity gets the best of me, so I go for it. "You are excited we are dating, right?" I hold my hands between my crossed legs, doubting myself.

"Of course!" He reaches for my hand. "I am happy you're here and I'm more than excited to continue this journey with you. You're so special to me and they're going to love you and love us." I smile and nod. He pulls me a little closer to give me a kiss, sending chills down my spine. "I will tell them today. Let's go in. I promise it's in the works."

As we head for the door, Toby gives me a quick kiss on the cheek while first reassuring we are alone. "Have you ever been laser tagging?" he asks.

With excitement, I say, "Yeah, who hasn't? I quite enjoy it, actually. Y'all are going to get your asses kicked."

"Oh, you're talking a big game here. We will see!" He opens the door for me and I walk in. A plethora of overwhelming noises come from every direction of the building.

Bright lights flash from arcade games, a mixture of concession smells fills my nostrils, and people uncontrollably run amok. I see Toby connect with a group of people sitting on a bench across the black-and-neon-carpeted lobby area. They welcome us with smiles all around, standing up to hug us as well. Toby watches each hug and targets me before we even start the game, teasing, "Wow, those are some good hugs!"

Laughing at the inside joke, I ask, "Oh, you want one too?"

He nods his head, replying, "Of course I do." As I go in for the hug, his arms reach around my waist as opposed to my neck, as he normally would. He makes it a weak, quick touch while I wrap his head in my arms, essentially suffocating him.

Annie, Kevin, and Brock all chuckle while Toby holds a huge, cheesy grin on his face. "Since the crew is all here and acquainted, shall we make a move to the concession area so I can get my ICEE on?" Kevin can't hold back his excitement any longer.

We walk to a gray tabletop with a neon squiggle pattern that matches with the floor of the concession area, where Annie kicks off the conversation. She asks me, "Keith, do you go to OSU as well? What are you studying?" These are on brand for her first questions. Toby mentioned her purity, but he failed to mention how it just radiates off her. She's short with dark hair and blue eyes and her style gives me Jess-from-*New Girl* vibes while her personality screams straight-A worrywart.

We get our red and blue ICEEs and make our way to a table as I answer, "I go to University of Cincinnati and am a marketing major. It was an easy choice with the scholarship offer and because I was born and raised there." We all sit down at a table, getting comfortable.

"Incredible. I'm on scholarship too," Annie replies.

Kevin adds, "Yeah, you're a genius, Annie. Who actually knows what they want in life. No one our age knows they want to be a divorce counselor at our age. I mean, I'm glad you know, but baby, you're top tier in our class. No doubt. Most people just go to college to figure out what's next." Kevin nearly begs to be relatable. I could just be jealous of his past with my boyfriend, but it seems he is trying to impress him. Either he did dress up for the occasion, *or* I'm a jealous bitch and he simply cares about the way he's perceived. Either way, he's good looking and has impeccable style—you can't go wrong with Chuck Taylors and a bomber jacket.

"What are you in school for, Kevin?" I ask.

"Accounting. It's always intrigued me but not sure if it's something I'll do for the rest of my life. These days, as long as you have a degree, you're in the clear." We all agree.

"It's also so much more applicable to all jobs, as opposed to, I don't know, engineering. Seems niche to me," I say.

Brock sits back in his chair with his blond hair pushed back and his arms crossed. "I'm in engineering," he replies with a grimace. We all laugh while Brock just holds a barely passable smile.

"Wait, how do you all know each other?" I ask to feel out the vibe.

Kevin looks around for someone to answer, but Annie signals for him to go. "Well, Brock and I are in a fraternity together, but we both met Toby prior without knowing. One day, Toby and I were eating in the student cafeteria and saw Brock. We all got to talking and planned to hang out—the rest is history." Holding eye contact with Kevin, I nod while he continues. "Toby brought Annie around a few times and I've been obsessed with her since she made the joke about pulling a chicken wing through the gap in her teeth to get all the meat off."

She smiles, the gap clear as day, and sits back while saying, "Charles Darwin would be so proud," happy as can be.

Toby and I begin laughing uncontrollably, getting everyone a little riled up. Toby begins leaning on the table with his arms underneath reaching for my leg. At the same time he asks, "How did you never tell me this? That is hilarious."

Brock stands up and announces, "I'm going to use the restroom." As I watch him walk, I notice his fresh, relaxed athletic wear. He stands slightly taller than me, a little above six feet and pretty thin.

"What's his deal?" Annie asks, then turns in my direction. "Sorry, he isn't usually this way. Something must be up."

"Don't apologize to me; I'm having a good time," I reply with a smile on my face.

"Me too. Let's go to the arena when he gets back. We can make the next time slot," Toby suggests. We all agree while slurping down our ICEEs to the finish.

"I feel bad for whoever gets stuck with us." They all share a laugh. I continue, "But I must say, I don't get the hype around these ICEEs. They taste normal to me." I throw shade to get under Kevin's skin.

Kevin retorts, "Normal never tasted so good."

* * *

While lining up in a dark, rectangular waiting room, ample televisions loop an instructional video as we chat and laugh over the projected sound. In short order, an employee enters the room to give additional instructions. We patiently listen as he forces us to watch the video, and then, as directed, we each grab a vest at random.

Each lights up with a specific color, which determines the teams. Toby, Kevin, and I turn red as our vests light up, while Annie and Brock light up in blue. We see the competition and start taunting each other as the instructor joins in, asking everyone, "Are you ready?"

The door opens to the arena, a cloud of cold air hits me in the face, and we proceed. Once we walk through the doorway, the space opens up to an overwhelming two-story room. It's only lit by black light to illuminate the neon green-and-orange tape lining the objects in the room. The back of the room holds two neon green enclosures that sit about twenty feet away from one another, which house stairways inside. A knotted rope bridge links the enclosures to each other, while the rest of the arena hides behind hollow cubes and flat neon walls.

A digital clock sits on the wall above the knotted bridge, counting down in red numbers. We are given a few minutes to set up before the shooting begins. Everyone splits up except for Kevin and me. We start in one of the hollow cubes. The buzzer sounds and instantly the lasers shoot all over the place. The lasers' strange, warped buzzing sound fills my ears, making it difficult to adjust.

Kevin leans over my shoulder and yells in my ear over the noise. "We never discussed this but are we taking this seriously as a whole team with the randoms, or are we just worried about our group?"

We switch places as I say, "Let's just keep it between us. I'm not sure how we will keep score that way but with three against two, it should be a no brainer."

He agrees and motions his head to exit the cube. Before exiting, I glance through the window of the cube. My eyes lock on Brock, who walks into one of the stairways leading to the bridge.

Kevin quickly fades the blue on Annie's vest with a direct shot.

"What a cheap shot, Kevin!" Annie yells and begins to go after him while waiting for her vest to activate again.

Ditching him, I run to the bridge. I see Toby sitting on the tower's stairs while Brock stands in front of him. Toby's face seems rather serious and concerned. I hide behind the opposite tower.

Maybe he's telling Brock about us?

They didn't see me, so I make an attempt to get closer, hiding behind the stairs of their tower. I can't make out what they're saying while the lasers blare in every direction. I can't get close enough. I make my way around the stairs to take my courtesy shot at Brock and watch the blue fade from his chest.

I breeze past them and continue hunting Annie. I must have broken up their powwow because Toby startles me, wrapping his arms around me soon thereafter.

"What were you and Brock talking about?" I yell into his ear.

He lets out a deep breath, seemingly overwhelmed. "I'll tell you about it in the car."

* * *

"You all had three people and still lost. Kevin was cheating, too. He always runs up from behind and shoots," Annie taunts after the blue team is deemed victorious.

Kevin replies, "We need the stats broken down per player. No way you all beat us."

"Okay, we may have lost at laser tag but I will beat all of you at this basketball game over here," Toby says as he walks away from the group.

Annie nudges me to come with her to the pinball machine. I begin getting to know her on our walk over, asking, "Did you grow up here?"

"I did—my whole family has. I just love it here so much. It has changed a lot though, quite recently."

"How so?"

"Well, my parents got a divorce a couple years ago and my younger sister isn't taking it well." I present an obligatory apology regarding the divorce. "That's sweet, Keith. It's truly better this way. Nonetheless, I want to become a divorce counselor to help kids in my little sister's position have an easier transition."

"I'm sure your sister looks up to you quite a bit. She has a great role model!"

Annie stops playing pinball to look at me. "Thank you, that truly means a lot."

Toby approaches at the perfect time to give Annie a hug. "I'm ready to head out. I am one tired, sore loser."

Annie and I laugh. We exchange another hug and "nice to meet yous." Kevin and Brock approach and we say our goodbyes. Acting overly nice, Kevin tells me, "It was great to meet you. I know we won; we were doing so well. Maybe we can all hang out again soon." He gives me a firm hug. Upon its release I find myself facing Brock.

I force a smile on my face and say, "It's been a pleasure. I had a good time."

"Same. See you soon," Brock says as we exchange a quick, obligatory hug.

Toby looks back and waves as we walk away. Upon exiting the doors, we quickly regain the ability to hear ourselves think again. I exclaim, "I had a blast!"

Toby agrees and asks, "Aren't they the best?"

I turn to him, replying, "I really enjoy Annie. I've never met such a perfect soul. Kevin makes me laugh and seems like a good guy. I didn't really get the best read on Brock. He gave me standoffish vibes. Does that have something to do with your conversation during the game?"

Toby opens my car door while answering the question. "Brock noticed when I rubbed your leg at the concession area, so I told him we were dating."

Once he gets in the car, I bombard him with questions. "This being good or bad? How did he respond? Did his pouting stem from rubbing my leg?" My stomach becomes a little anxious to hear what Toby has to say.

"It's great!" Not what I expected him to say. "I told him we are dating and I'm happy. I mentioned things were going in a really great direction." He begins to drive the car and puts his hand on my thigh.

"Nice. A good step, right? Are you okay? You don't sound too over the moon about it."

"I am." He laughs, "I didn't mean to sound unenthusiastic. Brock just isn't over our past. So when he saw us, it upset him." We pull up to a stop light. He pulls my head over and we kiss at the red light. "When we were on the stairs, I basically told him he would be seeing a lot of you so he needed to make a change in his demeanor. That's it. I definitely got the point across."

"How has he held onto this for so long without even mentioning it to you?" I question. "Seems strange."

"I know; I am also taken back. We are just friends and have been for a while." We pause. "Well, I had a good time tonight and everyone enjoyed you, so there's one win on our docket."

"Except Brock," I clap back, jokingly.

"Stop. You won't hear about him anymore. I promise," Toby reassures me. I trust him and lean my head over on his shoulder. He pulls it closer.

When we arrive back to room 317, the exhaustion kicks in, but so do more questions about his past with Brock.

Should I have more suspicions regarding Toby and Brock? Would Toby just tell me this to make me happy? Toby hasn't given me any reason not to trust him.

My head spins with what-ifs.

I do trust him. I want this to work. How do I get to know more without sounding crazy about it?

We fall asleep before I figure out the best way to ask.

CH. 8

WALKING AWAY

——

Since I failed to address the Brock situation the night of, I neglect to bring it up again to avoid sounding insane to Toby. For now, I decide Toby can deal with the mess he made; I'm sure he has it under control.

Regardless, Toby was there for me through some emotional and major moments in my life up to this point and I truly appreciate and admire him all the more for it. As it has become a regular part of our relationship, I devise a plan to surprise him with something special, as a thank you for driving down after Tailgate, getting me out of Cincinnati for the last few weekends, and for ultimately helping me discover myself.

To casually gather some information, I send him a simple text: "Hi beebee! What are you doing this weekend? I have to work Saturday morning and Sunday night. Do you think a trip here for the evening could be possible so I can see you briefly?"

"I have plans with Annie on Saturday night. A new restaurant is opening downtown and Annie wants to test it out. I would feel bad to cancel. We have been talking about this for weeks," Toby deflects.

"Oh, no no. Don't cancel. Go see Annie. You know I adore her."

After this conversation, I do some investigative work. Searching through Toby's profile, I find his friends and quickly pinpoint Annie's page. I shoot her a message:

"Hey Annie! I had the best time at our laser tag night, we will have to do it again soon. But maybe you could help me with a little surprise this weekend. I know you and Toby have plans so I wanted to know more about those before I made any arrangements. I didn't want to blow my cover, so asking Toby didn't make sense to me. Anyway, I don't want to interfere, just plan around. Also, let's keep this between us!"

I know I can trust Annie.

In my search of what to surprise Toby with, I think of some options. I know Toby played soccer growing up and loved to play. I specifically remember the day he realized he missed the sign-up deadline for the intramural soccer league at school.

* * *

We were on the phone between classes while he stood by a community board in the hall. "Chess club? Ew, I'm awful at chess. Woman's rights march... I can dig it—nope, I'm busy Saturday with my beebee. Queer book club... if only I felt comfortable. Oh! Soccer! I can do this one."

"You should sign up! I'll come watch every game," I encouraged him.

"No! I missed the deadline." He made a depressive moaning noise. "Maybe I can just ask kindly—this was five weeks ago. Who is in charge of updating these boards? They aren't doing a good job," he jokes, despite his disappointment.

* * *

With this memory in mind, I notice the Columbus Crew's "Black & Gold" showcase game online. *We have to go.*

"Annie... Hello, where are you? I need answers, girly," I say out loud to my phone.

As if she heard me, my phone vibrates with a reply from Annie. I laugh at myself as I open the message. "Hi Keith! Wow, he would love a little surprise! Tell me everything. I don't remember us making plans, but I will double check with him." Annie wants to help—perfect.

"Oh! He said you were all going to a restaurant you've been eager to try on Saturday. Ring any bells?" I ask.

"I have been wanting to go to a few places. I wonder which one it could be. I will get to the bottom of it. What are you thinking of surprising him with?"

"Please keep it a secret! I convinced him I have to work this weekend so I could buy us tickets to the Crew Black & Gold game."

"My lips are sealed. He will love it so much. You all are such sweet friends to each other! How can I help pull this off?"

Hmm. Friends? She must really be oblivious.

"Ugh! You're the best. If you want to join, I can get you a ticket, too! It can be a family affair; we can ask Brock and Kevin," I respond.

"I think Brock has to work at the diner and Kevin has plans with his family. Looks like it's just you two, I don't do sports (:"

Perfect! Annie forgot about their plans; tickets are in my inbox. This is going smoothly—almost too smooth.

My thoughts turn sour. *Should I be concerned he never had plans with Annie? Did he have plans with someone else? Damn, stop thinking this way, Keith!*

* * *

"Have a good day, bee. I hope you have fun tonight with Annie." I shoot Toby a text upon arriving in Columbus.

"Thank you. If something changes, I will let you know and maybe I can just drive down to you. Hopefully she cancels. I really want to see you." Little does he know, she already canceled.

"Be careful what you wish for (;"

"Who do I talk to about my three wishes? It's time to redeem wish number one, please." He adds a little genie emoji.

"I might be able to make all of your dreams come true. Some call me a therapist while others call me Magic Mike. Only time will reveal the truth here." I send him a double text. "What are you going to do until dinner?"

"Magic Mike, come to me! I'll lay here alone, I guess. Am I going to spend my life waiting for our schedules to align?"

"If you know what's good for you, you will," I taunt him.

As we continue bantering, I acquire a pair of Columbus Crew shirts to sport at the game, along with some of his favorite Max & Erma cookies and a gift bag. But packaging gifts in a car is harder than anticipated. The black and gold bag sits in the passenger seat while I terribly fold the shirts on my lap. I resort to shoving them in the bag and placing the cookies on top.

As any professional does, I fluff white tissue paper to the perfect wrinkle-to-fold ratio and ensure the goods are covered.

* * *

I pull up to the garage on campus and text Toby. "Hi Tobee. Where are you?"

"My dorm. What's up? Want to FaceTime 'cause you miss me? :)"

"You have a delivery for you downstairs," I text back, making my way to the front to plant the bag in the perfect spot.

"What? Really? I didn't order anything. Lol."

Just to the side of the main doors, I place the bag in front of a line of bushes. "Go to the lobby door, baby."

"Did you order a pizza or something?"

"Lol. It's a very *special* pizza delivery." He calls me after this text and I hear some ruffling and the door to his dorm slam.

"Who's downstairs?" he questions with anticipation.

I cackle, "Just go look. You'll be pleasantly surprised. Are you already on your way down?"

"Just getting dressed."

"Oh I heard a slam, thought it might be the door closing behind you."

"Yeah... Paul just walked out of the door."

"Nice!" I make my way around the corner of the building to the side door. As I look around, I see someone walking away from the dorm facing the garage. His back side is visible enough for me to make out his thin figure and blonde hair. He has a nice, fitted style, which causes me to pause and wonder, *Wait, was that... No... I don't think so.* Maybe my eyes are playing tricks on me, but that looked like...

"Hello? Did you just get distracted?" Toby asks after my extended silence, pulling me from my train of thought.

"I did, sorry. This person I just saw looked familiar."

I hear the elevator ding. "Do you know them? Okay, I'm almost outside." He opens the door to the front of the dorm with no one around. "Keith, I don't see anyone. Are you sure they're at my building?"

Ignoring his question, I peer around the corner and see him looking around for anyone in sight. "Look in front of the line of bushes."

The black and gold bag looks as if it just emerged from the bushes. "What are you doing to me? Does this contain a glitter bomb?"

"No, it doesn't, but I'll save that idea."

"Who put this here?" His confusion hits.

"I told you a special pizza guy delivered it for you." I begin to turn the corner and I see him looking through the bag a little.

Toby grows silent. "No you didn't. How would you do that?" He hears the grass brush against my black shoes and looks in my direction. "Keith! What are you doing here?" A big smile appears on his face! As he runs over, he drops his smile but still goes in for a weak hug. "Why aren't you at work?" He peers behind me, as if looking for another surprise.

"Just had a forethought out week. It was all for the surprise, bee. Did you see what's in here?"

"Yes, I did. Are you trying to fatten me up? I love these cookies. But what are the shirts for? I haven't taken them out yet."

"For you to pick which one you want to wear tonight."

"To what exactly? Annie and I have plans."

"Not anymore. Well, she forgot you had plans so she gave you to me for the evening. She's been helping me plan our night at the Black & Gold game."

"You can't be serious!" He pulls the black shirt from the bag in shock and looks up at me with a pure glow on his face. He slaps my arm with the bag and says, "I can't believe this. I have been talking about this game since... for forever! I've always wanted to go. I didn't think we talked about it, did we?"

"I just thought you might enjoy it. We play soccer a lot and I had a hunch you might love it. I just wanted to show my appreciation for putting up with my drama over the last few weeks."

"Bee, you're so sweet but you know you don't have to thank me." I shake my head, disagreeing. "Come upstairs. I'm glad Paul went home for the weekend."

"Didn't Paul just leave?"

"Yeah... to go home."

"Oh, right, okay." *Hmm, would I have seen him leave?* "How's your weekend? Did you hang out with Kevin and Brock last night?" I investigate as we board the elevator.

He knocks his knuckle on the wood as it takes us up. "Yeah, we just played some board games. Nothing crazy." Upon entering 317, I race to the restroom while Toby makes his way to the bedroom and rummages around a bit. I push the door open to the bedroom while I wash my hands.

"What are you doing in there? Sounds like a damn tornado." Peering around the door frame, Toby quickly makes his bed and picks some clothes up off the floor, moving them to his laundry basket.

"Just cleaning up a bit. Sorry, look at this place. It's a wreck. What time does the game start, anyway?" Toby changes the subject as his eyes scan the room for more unorganized messes.

"We have two hours before it starts. It isn't too far away, but I figured we would get dinner before."

"And Annie doesn't mind?"

"Yes, I invited her to be nice but she said she 'doesn't know how to sports.' She didn't even remember you had plans. We can invite her again, if you want." I approach my boyfriend and pull him in for a kiss. "She may get in the way, you know?"

"Oh, yeah. Let's—" I interrupt with another kiss as he continues, "not."

"Mmm," I slightly moan as he fully removes his weight from his feet and transfers it onto me. His legs are wrapped around my thighs. I manage to walk over to the bed without removing his tongue from my throat, gently laying him on the bed and crawling over him.

I can feel his excitement, mostly through his shorts. We begin to push boundaries we haven't pushed before—baby steps though. "Let's not get too carried away," he says.

"Babe, I'm fully following your lead, Mr. Wrap Your Legs Around Me. We don't *have* to stop," I suggest.

"We've been messing around for thirty minutes. We both need to get cleaned up," he suggests as he tries to wiggle his way out from under me.

Feeling misled, I look around to find the closest clock. I reach for Toby's phone as it's the closest—he also reaches for it after noticing me. "Whoa, thirty minutes went by fast! I wish we had time for another thirty. And look who killed the mood: Brock called you three times."

I suddenly realize Brock was definitely who I saw earlier. *He doesn't live here, does he? Fuck, I hate this.*

"Oh, he probably just remembered something funny and feels the need to tell me. He does that from time to time and acts like it's important."

Likely story.

CH. 9

SLOW DOWN

Fans decked out in black and gold jam-pack the lower level of the stands. The venue resembles most football stadiums, with an open ceiling allowing the beautiful daylight to flow in. As we find our seats, the teams run from concrete tunnels on the opposite corners of the field. Towels swing in the air and pompoms shake everywhere as the announcer hypes up the crowd. The smell of beefy hot dogs and popcorn fill the air, the combination of which create an impeccable vibe.

As we locate our seats in the nosebleeds, I point out how "the website made row DD sound a lot better." I can see the field, which is all I need. He's giddy just to be here, or so I thought. Row DD and the surrounding seats have fans scattered around, so it's spacious up here.

"You're going to have to keep me in the loop when they throw the cards because I can't keep up. I didn't really play any sports involving balls growing up," I say while laughing. Although Toby tests me quite a bit when we play at the intramural fields to teach me some rules, I still feel uneducated.

"No worries, I played for years. I got you, bee," he says with a slight pat on the leg, which still riles me up in public. Those subtle hints of "I wish I could touch you more" mean a lot knowing we aren't completely comfortable being together in public yet, so it's a step in the right direction.

Not to mention, we are both traumatized from years of negative slurs and the hatred for the gay community. We're young and still learning what works for us and what doesn't, and that's okay.

We begin to focus on the game. I lean my elbows on my knees in the faded gray seat while straightening my back. Toby begins in the same position and shifts as time passes, leaning back in his chair with his legs wide open.

The game progresses and I, of course, don't know what's going on. A card flashes in the air and the ball shifts possession. I look to Toby for the answers. "What just happened?"

"What happened? I wasn't looking," he replies.

"I'm not sure. He flashed a red card and somehow the gold team magically acquired the ball. But everything looked normal."

"If they'd play the replay, I could tell you." But they never do.

"Oh well. I guess it doesn't really matter." I return to my stance and continue watching. As the game progresses, I begin seeing a pattern of me having to ask what happened in the game and Toby barely paying enough attention to explain.

Finally, I lean back in my seat, asking, "Are you okay?"

"Yeah, why?"

"You don't seem engaged in the game," I point out.

"I'm watching." He smiles and laughs, trying to play it off. "I'm also talking to Kevin about the semester ending and where I'm going to live. Just a little stressed about moving in with Auntie Amanda."

"Oh, why are you so stressed?"

Bzzz.

We both can't help but look down at his phone. The name I see definitely doesn't start with a K, but maybe he just received a different text. "She just isn't the cleanest and I want to keep my belongings tidy. She makes me feel burdensome anytime I even ask a question. I could think of many places I would rather go."

"You'll have your own space, won't you?"

"I will."

"Just make it your own and stay in there. Keep it clean and it'll be a nice little escape. You can come to Cincinnati whenever you'd like, you know?" I try to comfort him.

"Thank you. It'll be okay; it's just for the summer, until Paul and I get our own apartment when he comes back next semester."

"You'll have a refreshing space to make your own. Exciting, right?" I grab his knee to comfort him and ask, "Do you want anything from the concession stand?"

"I'm okay; thank you, bee." I proceed to get up and make my way to the lower end of the stairs. I look up to see Toby writing a novel on his phone, yet again.

In an attempt to let my frustrations simmer down, I carry on with my adventure for a Dr. Pepper.

I parade back up the stairs, soda in hand, but Toby doesn't even notice. He jumps when my voice projects in such close proximity, "Are you ready to watch the game?"

"You scared me. Yes, let's watch!"

I proceed to sit down and situate the large Dr. Pepper I acquired. *Did I take him away from something today? Surely he would have brought it up. If he's texting Brock, this stadium will know how pissed I am. What are the odds it's actually Kevin?*

Bzzz.

Focus shifts before the ball can even make it to the next player. He returns to his texts.

I stand and bend over to gather my belongings. "I'm ready to go."

"What? The game's not over."

"It seems you're too busy for this today. You have a lot on your mind so let's go take care of that." I avoid eye contact and head for the stairs.

He watches as I exit row DD. He begins to gather his things from the chair and eventually catches up to me down the stairs, asking, "Why are you mad?"

"Frustrated, really." We head down the stairs and exit the stadium in silence while maintaining a nice duckling formation.

As we enter the blacktop parking lot, I gain some ground and Toby attempts to catch up to me once again. "Can you slow down?" he pleads.

I stop. "Sure. Are you ready to talk to me? Wait, make sure Kevin hasn't texted you first."

"I have been talking to you."

"Oh yeah, I forgot the *one*, singular conversation we had during a whole soccer game"—my sarcasm is very apparent at this point—"where I am trying to show you I appreciate and care for you. I went through hoops to make this special for you and you don't give a damn, dude." He doesn't say anything.

When get in the car, I cross my arms, face the window, and slouch on the black leather interior seat. He reaches over and rubs my leg a little. "Hey."

I'm not having it in the slightest, pushing his hand off me. "Could you just drive, please."

The car begins to move. "Kevin messaged me about—"

"You weren't talking to Kevin." I cut him off, talking over him with the most confidence possible. "I saw Brock leave your dorm and I saw he called you. Don't lie. Did you have plans with Brock today? Since Annie"—I add air quotes—"forgot about your *so-called* plans."

"Truthfully, I'm talking to Kevin. You can see."

I finally crank my neck in his direction. "I don't want to see. I want you to tell me and to believe you. I simply did this to show you my appreciation." I take my tone down a notch. "You know how the gay community works. For all I know, you two are probably still hooking up. Shit, between Kevin and Brock, I don't know who you're more obsessed with." I take a breather. "This is the way our society is—and you've given me no reason to believe you are any different than the rest of the community."

Toby finally gets the balls to defend himself, calmly. "Kevin and I aren't anything. He just needed to talk to me and I want my friends to know I'm here for them. He's always been there for me."

"I'm not trying to take your friends away; I'm trying to find my place in your life. It's just odd because you don't spend time on your phone any other day, but today you had to." We pull off the interstate and inch closer to campus.

"If your friends were texting you—"

"Toby, I don't care about your excuses and Kevin's problems. You're failing to realize what it takes to make a relationship work. We don't have secrets, we include one another, and offer to help each other's friends. Don't you think my opinion would have been valuable from a different perspective?"

"I didn't want to tell you his business. It's not my business to tell."

"Okay, Toby. If you really don't trust me enough to keep his secret then it's a matter of saying, 'I'm with Keith at a soccer game. Let's talk later.' What's so hard about saying either of those things?" He stays silent. "Can you drop me off at my car, please? I'm just going to head home. Sounds like Kevin needs you."

* * *

Bzzz.

I barely make it out of the city before Toby calls me. I ignore it.

Bzzz.

"Please, it's an emergency." Toby sends me a text. He tugs at my heartstrings. Do I fall for this?

Bzzz.

He calls again. In my most stern voice I answer, "Hello."

"I got in a wreck. Will you please come get me?"

"Shit…" My guilt starts to hit. "Are you serious?"

"Yes, I'm sending you my location. Will you come?"

I lower my voice and say, "Of course. Are you okay?"

"I might need stitches in a couple places. The ambulance is pulling up. Text me your ETA… And thank you, for everything today." We hang up the phone and I pull up the directions to his location.

"I'll be there in ten," I text him.

I arrive at the usually busy intersection. I see the blue and red lights flashing and a few cars using turning lanes to go around the accident under the traffic lights. I pull into a parking lot on the corner and stand on the curb with my arms crossed. Toby sees me and I send a measly wave by barely lifting my hand from my bicep.

A tow truck proceeds to pull the Corolla onto its platform. In the process, I observe the front passenger headlight dangling out of place, the front bumper hanging down, the hood cranking back, and the tire turning inward. Realizing the significance of the accident, I stand patiently thinking about the last things I said to him.

I'm an asshole.

* * *

I wrap my arms around Toby's waist, as gently as I can. He looks at me, his eyes glossed over. "I'm sorry. You were absolutely right; I should have paid attention to you. When I dropped you off, I missed you as soon as you closed the car door and realized I acted foolish. I don't want you to leave." I go in to move his bloody head into the light. He retreats, admitting, "Ow... I rejected the ambulance ride because I didn't want to pay for it, but they think I need stitches."

"Stitches for your head?" I say in shock. Moving his head back and forth to get the light in the right spot, I reassure him, "It doesn't look too bad."

My body turns 180 degrees to face the same direction as Toby does, to head to Hauni. I rest my hand on his lower back to reassure him it would be okay. Afterward, I open the passenger door for him and he takes a seat. I run over to the driver's side and take my place. "How did this happen?"

"Yeah, the yellow light didn't last as long as I had anticipated. By the time I sped up and got to the light, I couldn't slow down to a complete stop, so I had to go for it. I barely hit the intersection as the light changed. The other car jumped ahead of their green light, when it was still technically red.

Both of us were really at fault, but I take blame for being such an idiot."

"Where were you going in such a hurry?" I say, trying to pry information from him.

He looks over at me and says, "Following you, or trying to. You were going pretty fast."

"Me? What? Why were you following me?"

"Well... I realized I didn't want you to go and didn't have the courage to call and apologize, yet. I figured if it meant I had to drive all the way to Cincinnati to do it, then I'd have no choice at that point." He's rambling and I catch him smiling. I do too, but I'm still trying to act mad.

I avoid giving him the satisfaction. "Do you think you need to go to the hospital? I can take you there," I offer, to distract from my small smile.

"I'll be okay. They're just being dramatic. Do you think I need any?"

"It doesn't seem deep to me. Do you feel okay?" I ask to be sure.

"I'm more than okay since you're here. I'm sorry I ruined our day, but thank you for coming. Will you stay with me?"

I grab his hand, pull it to my lips, and plant a soft kiss on it. "You didn't ruin the day. We just wrote another chapter in our book, babe. Yes, I'll stay."

CH. 10

MCDONALD'S CUPS & CIGARETTE BUTTS

"I can't believe you were coming after me. That's cute as shit!" I begin the early morning chat. He smiles at me with confidence. "I'm sorry. The thought of you and Brock just overwhelms me. I don't want to think this way but unfortunately the way I grew up created this fear."

"I'm not upset at you. I'm sorry, too. You are my focus, bee. Yesterday, distractions got in the way. I should have been more present and I appreciate the thought you put into the day."

"It didn't quite go as planned."

"I know, and I'm sorry I messed it up." He bats his eyes and gives me pure puppy dog sap. "I've endured enough punishment, if I do say so myself. I lost the love of my life: my baby Corolla."

"Oh," I chuckle, "the love of your life, huh?"

"Shit, am I in trouble again?" Pulling me closer with morning breath galore, he says, "We have to trust each other.

My friends are just friends. I promise there's nothing to worry about. You can't create those scenarios."

"I just needed the confirmation—again." We shut our eyes. "Growing pains hurt the most."

Just as I am about to fall asleep for a nap, Toby rolls over, breaking the silence. "I had a weird dream last night." He continues as my eyes slowly open, "It seemed I moved everything to Aunt Amanda's and had my dog, Brachi, with me."

"Uh oh," I interject. "Tell me more. Also, I love your dog's name."

"Yes! Brachi, like the dinosaur! Anyway, out of nowhere, everything keeps multiplying and growing bigger, quickly filling my room. Brachi disappears, swallowed whole by boxes and books, and I am sitting and watching as I just grow smaller, kind of acclimating myself to the space. Eventually, I keep getting smaller, but everything around me dissolves and I end up on the street with all my original boxes. Strange, right?"

"Damn. Toby, it can't be healthy to have this weighing on your mind. Have you asked if you could stay yet?" Toby shakes his head from side to side. "Babe, maybe you should just call her to make sure she's okay with it before it's too late to find another plan. Are you more scared of being on the street or the clutter in her house?"

"Oh gosh, can I say both?" He laughs. "I don't know. I just have to do it."

"Pick up the phone and call her now. Get it out of the way," I demand.

"Yes sir." While saluting, Toby picks up the phone, dialing Auntie Amanda on speaker.

"Hey," she answers, unamused.

"Hi Auntie Amanda! I wanted to run something by you."
He pauses for an answer, which doesn't seem to come. "I've
been thinking about the summer. I want to keep my job at
the library for my resume and I want to stay near campus.
Since you live in town, I wanted to ask if I could stay with
you for a few months, until my lease starts in the fall."

"Why do you want to keep a shit-paying job anyway, Toby?
Get you a money-making job," Auntie Amanda claps back.

"I've *told* you. Since I'll be in education, it will look good
on my resume for postgraduation and getting a job in the
school system here." She doesn't say anything. "I won't be
there a lot. I will be in Cincinnati on the weekends and I will
work most of the time I'm in town, or I'll be with friends. It's
basically for my things to sit until August." He makes a fair
attempt at convincing her it would be fine.

"When would you move your crap here?"

"After finals. So, the middle of May."

"Okay, Toby. Fine."

"Thank you! We will have a good time."

"Mm-hmm. Bye." She hangs up the phone.

Toby turns to look at me. "Well... better than expected."

* * *

Toby fights through nerves; the day has arrived for him to
move out of the dorm and into Auntie Amanda's place. I vol-
unteer to help, partly to spend more time with my boyfriend,
but more so because he won't ask anyone else for help.

All of Toby's belongings lie on the sidewalk outside of
his red brick dorm, which he accompanies, standing there
waiting for my arrival. Once he notices Hauni come down
the street, he begins flaring one arm, resembling Forrest

Gump with his hand on his back hip. I pull next to the freshly fixed-from-the-wreck Corolla and step out of the car in my workout clothes and running shoes.

Ironically, Toby is wearing my favorite blue shirt. "You know this shirt means a lot to me," I say.

"How so?" Toby asks as he comes in for a hug and kiss.

"Well, it's in the Instagram photo I show everyone when they ask who I am seeing. You also wore it when we first met over there," I explain, pointing at the garage I first parked in.

"Wow, you are adorable. I love this sentimental side of you." Toby compliments me. "It probably looks awful on me now; I put on some pounds," he says while slapping his belly.

"Shut up, cotton shirts shrink so much. I would know if you've gained weight, baby. You look just as great as the first time I laid eyes on you—just with a smaller shirt." We laugh together as he begins directing which car gets which boxes.

I come across a box of plush animals and start to look through them. Pulling out a T-Rex, I move his little arms and throw him at Toby. "Oh god," he says, as I sense his embarrassment. "I knew you were going to find the damn animal box. It's just all my toys from when I grew up. I didn't trust anyone to keep them." My heartstrings feel a tug.

As we move everything from the curb, Toby thanks me with a kiss. "I guess just follow me. I'll send the address in case you can't keep up," he adds.

The Corolla heads out and I follow. I have spent my fair share of time in Columbus but have never been to the outskirts where Auntie Amanda lives. After getting out of the city limits, we drive down narrow roads, McDonald's cups and cigarette butts lining their sides along with other trash. The trees are just sporadic enough to see the run-down, small, single-level, vinyl homes that have moss growing all over, which adds to the aesthetic.

We pull off the main road into the neighborhood where the trees clear up a bit, only to reveal the same style homes, with less land and a touch of brick around the main living room window. Toby's blinker signals a turn and I anxiously inspect every house for the next ten down to see which one we pull into.

I see the silver Corolla pull into a cracked, oil-stained driveway with weeds running rampant in the cracks. Clearly, nobody edges their grass in this neighborhood, and, oh boy, maybe Aunt Amanda missed trash day a couple times this month, or even this year. The garbage cans and excess bags cover the red brick around the living room window. A single-stepped, cracked concrete porch holds ample cigarette butts, ashes, and luckily two foldable, previously white chairs in front of the house. The screen door hangs wide open while the front door holds an oval-shaped glass window. A *cute* dirt ombre pattern covers the door. The remainder of the home has yellow vinyl panels wrapping around the side while the gutter has become overrun by sticks and leaves.

Toby pulls into the driveway while I park on the road in the front. As I park, the ombre door opens and a pink sleep shirt sneaks out with a floating head holding a cigarette in its lips. Unable to make out what she says while she comes out yelling, a mid-sized, scraggly gray dog runs out with its tail blazing. I look to Toby to find his gorgeous smile ear to ear while he kneels to squeeze the incredibly happy little mutt. Toby stands while tilting his head to the side and pulling his shoulder to his ear, saying, "Hi Auntie Amanda. How has Brachi been doing? Look how excited she looks!"

"She best be happy. That lil' shit runs all over my house and sits on my recliner too damn much. Her food ain't cheap down the road there." Toby looks at me as I stand at my car. I can read the sorry from his eyes.

"Auntie Amanda, this is Keith. He's one of my friends from school and he's helping me move!"

"Hi Keith, good to meet you," she acts as if she gives a damn.

Of course, I smile and wave, replying, "So nice to meet you!"

Amanda returns to the house and goes about her day, not offering to help one bit. I turn to my car and begin to grab some small things. Before I can, Toby calls me over to show me around. As I approach the door, a waft of smoke smacks my face, neck, shoulder—everything. He looks back at me, mouthing the word "sorry" once more. I give him a pat on his little tush so he knows I'm okay.

Grass and dirt cover the vinyl landing pad. Upon entering the door, I take a look around while my nose adjusts to the utterly unique smell. The smoke and a musky moisture mixture becomes stronger the closer I get. I investigate the living room area, lit only by a lamp in the corner of the room. The yellow light hardly did its job, but it manages to light up the stains on the suede couch and the ashes in each crevice.

I noticed a slightly tilted frame on the wall. The original frame placement lines up perfectly with the discoloration in the paint. It sits just above a desk overtaken by boxes and papers, which are about to overtake the rest of the living space, too.

Toby continues to lead me to the room he now calls home. There sits a twin-sized bed with an older, detailed wooden bed frame, complete with linens, also discolored. Toby lets out a huge sigh as he begins to reach for his shadow, Brachi. Moving a box from the bed, he peers over at me. I approach him and scratch his back, telling him, "I'll go get some stuff from the car."

As I walk out the front door, Amanda emerges from the kitchen mumbling something and Toby appears from the hallway as I look back. I rummage through my car, picking up as many items as I can. Playing Tetris, I lose a box and it falls to the grass. I too drop to the grass to reorganize my items and head for the door.

As I approach the house, I hear Amanda getting louder: "Toby, if you don't like the way I live then you don't have to live here. You and your friend can move that shit somewhere else."

"I don't have anywhere to go," Toby says calmly. "I'm just asking if we can straighten up a bit before I get my stuff in here."

"I don't want you touching my stuff. It's all in its place. I know the location of everything I need." She's stern, clearly not wanting to make adjustments to her house. I sit the box down and take advantage of those white chairs on the porch. Toby doesn't yell but I can tell he begins to get frustrated while keeping his tone down.

"Auntie Amanda, do you hear yourself? You need the help. I just want to help you get organized; we don't have to get rid of anything."

"Toby, just 'cause you've gone off to college, you're not better than us. I am livin' just fine without your upper-class, educational brainwash bullshit."

"Me going to college has nothing to do with your well-being, Auntie Amanda. This isn't healthy and it could be beneficial if I was here to help sort it all." At this point, I realize we never made it past his room. I have no interest in seeing the condition of the bathroom and kitchen.

The dog runs out the open door and walks over to me, smells the box, and attempts jumping on my lap—I refuse. Focusing on Brachi, I scratch her little head while the argument fades into the back of the house.

Brachi perks her ears up, abruptly turning her head toward the noise as it resurfaces from the driveway. I do the same in an attempt to hear.

SLAM!

I jump out of the chair and stand up, waiting for someone to turn the corner.

"Just run to your brother. Have yourselves a homo little household together," Amanda yells from the back door, her voice echoing through the front lawn.

So uncalled for. What the hell just happened?

Toby turns the corner and says, "Come on, Keith." He's looking down, head tilted, tapping his leg. "Follow me. We're going to my brother's house." I scramble to grab the boxes from the porch and get back into my car.

BROTHERLY LOVE

———

The Corolla pulls out of the oily driveway while Brachi trots, following the car with her drooping ears. She's brokenhearted while watching us leave. I race to keep up with Toby. A sense of relief comes over me as his brake lights shine brightly in my face and Toby pulls into a driveway off the main road.

Rory stands on the porch in his Hanes socks, straight-legged jeans, and oversized Pokémon shirt. He's smiling, lighting up a cigarette. The duplex house sits on a corner lot. It has an interesting shape: the front porch wraps around two full sides while the back of the house holds no back doors or windows—it's just flat. The back corner holds the highest point of the home, allowing the roof to slant straight down to meet the porch's front corner. They love yellow siding in this town; it hugs Rory's house up to the gravel driveways on either side.

I get out of the car, approaching Toby sifting through his back seat. "Hey, are you okay? What happened back there?" I finally get to ask.

"Yes, I'm okay. I can't stay there, which I expected," he replies.

"Will you be staying here, then?"

"No, Rory said I could keep some stuff at his place. So let's unload your car here—I'm fairly certain I have everything I need day to day in mine. Well, I hope so, because this baby can't bear the thought of more cargo."

"Are you sure you don't need your plush toys?" I laugh to lighten the mood and I sense Toby's appreciation for it. "You sure you're okay?"

"Yeah, I knew her house wouldn't be livable for me. I assumed she would clean up a little, but clearly not. Sorry you had to witness our episode," he scoffs. "Thinking that would work in my favor was naive."

"Baby, it's okay. Can you just stay here with Rory?"

"I could sleep on the couch, but not with all his animals. I just can't for the whole summer. He just has extra closet space he doesn't really use, so he told me I could use it." I'm shocked at how he holds his composure so calmly, considering his homeless situation for the summer. "Just follow me and we can unload your car and get some food."

We each grab a box from my car and approach the porch. "Do I say I told you so now or later?" Rory taunts Toby in his dry tone. "I gave it more than thirty seconds, but even that was too much credit."

"Shut up, Rory. I have a plan; it's all good. This is Keith, my boyfriend." Toby introduces me.

I look at Toby, shocked he introduced me as his boyfriend, but, really, what reason does he have to hide anything from his brother? "Hey. How are you?" I greet Rory.

"I'm good, bub. I've heard good things about you."

He has?

"And thanks for watching after my brother after his accident. I'm glad you were with him. He told me all about it."

Wow, he tells Rory everything.

"I couldn't leave him there. Mostly because I had no choice." Rory laughs at my dig.

"Right! I would have left him a long time ago if I could. I'm stuck with him, but I'm not sure what the hell you're doing." Rory seems better than how Toby described him, although he might just be in a good mood.

"Are all of your animals put away, Rory?" Toby inquires, seemingly on a mission.

"They are, just for you baby brother!" Toby rolls his brown eyes at Rory.

I open my car door and grab the same box I've been moving for four hours. I follow Toby into the house. The only light comes from the heat lamps in the pet cages, which are able to illuminate the walkways. I walk by a shelf near the front window holding three cages. Rory begins to give me a tour and shows me all his pets. The snake, the tarantula, the lizards, the three dogs running around, a cat—I can't keep up with the rest. By the time I return to the car to help, one box remains. I grab it and turn back around to face the house, only for Toby to grab it, kiss me, and take it inside.

"I got it, baby," he says and turns back into the house.

"Well, good job, Keith. You managed to not do shit," Rory yells from the porch.

"Rory, come on. You were yapping about animal turds," I retort.

He laughs and says, "Don't act so uninterested. It's valuable information."

"Thank you for letting me keep some stuff here, Rory. We have to get going now." Toby interrupts our fun.

Saying our goodbyes to Rory. We walk to the car as I ask, "What now?"

Toby looks at me, takes a deep breath, and asks, "Do you want to get food?"

"That's the most romantic thing you've said all day. A nice pile of chicken, cheese, and rice sounds perfect."

He laughs and says, "I know just the place."

* * *

We roll up to this beautiful restaurant in a Walmart parking lot. The bottom half of the cement building is painted orange and the top half a light purple with no roof visible from the parking lot. Decrepit, clear plastic panels surround the patio to control outside weather. The cracked, unpainted parking lot comes fully equipped with a little green statue of a cactus near the road—a nice touch.

Upon entering the establishment, I find exactly what I had imagined—a little wooden podium with flags all around, colorful murals on the wall, and cheerful music; I can't wait for the salsa.

We sit, sharing a brief moment at the table to catch up on our texts while snacking on the chips. I begin to scroll through Instagram to find Lily and Blair in a dressing room, wrapping their legs around each side of some unstable poles holding a blue velvet curtain. "Wait! Are they at Pel Vintage?" I'm in shock. "How did they get an appointment at this place?"

"Can you not just book it online?" Toby asks in confusion.

"No, bee. Pel is the most exclusive vintage shop in Cincinnati. You have to be someone famous or know someone famous to get in. They don't open the doors to just anyone. They have the best vintage T-shirts and always have cool hats and pants. Ugh! I want to go."

Toby smiles and says, "You're crazy, bee. You should ask how they got in."

"It's okay, I'll have my chance one day." I grab Toby's hand and add, "Anyway, we're done with the hard part, right?"

He chuckles, replying, "Yes, thank you. I truly anticipated this happening. I have options, but don't know how to ask people for help."

"Of course, Columbus would be ideal but you know you can come to Cincinnati, don't you? Stay with me until you find somewhere to go."

"Really? I've had the thought, but I really don't want to move too quickly with you. I've seen Rory do it too many times, which is probably why he has had six boyfriends in the last two years." I shake my head, disregarding it as an abrupt notion. "I just enjoy what we have going on. I wouldn't want my situation to affect you too much. I mean, you've done more than enough."

"Toby, we aren't Rory. Truly, it'd be fine. You would be coming here for work a lot anyway and I'm going to have to work. We will make the best of it. I've grown fond of spending time with you. Besides, it's only temporary."

"If I could adjust my schedule at the library to only work Monday through Thursday, I could make it work. I can find a place to stay in Columbus during the week until I find something permanent." Toby brainstorms with me.

"That sounds great. Problem solved."

"I had it under control. I wasn't stressed." Toby's eyes quickly dart from side to side.

Smiling big, I admit, "I just didn't want your dreams of being homeless to come true. Excuse me for caring!" We share a laugh with a sigh of relief, for the time being.

CH. 12

RAWHIDE

"What do I write in this email to my boss? This kind of confrontation stresses me out." Overwhelmed and pulling on his hair, Toby paces through my room. "What if the library lets me go for requesting Monday through Thursday?" He's thinking out loud by the wood-paneled balcony door at my apartment. "I've been staying here a week now, so this will be giving them a two week notice."

"Plenty of time. At least you're offering something. You're giving them most of the week. No one even goes to the library on the weekends, do they? I mean it's summer." Toby shakes his head with confidence. "Let me type something up for you and see if you approve. At the end of the day they either say yes or no. They won't fire you; it's just a question."

"You're right. Not to mention, even if they are mad, they'll hopefully forget by the time classes start up," he replies.

"What are you going to do until then for work?" I made enough money to keep myself afloat, but I definitely was in no sugar daddy position at this stage of life.

"Oh!" Toby stops in his tracks. "I forgot to tell you, Brock got me a job at the diner he works at. I'm driving up tomorrow for an interview—well, not really any interview, more of a meet and greet and to get paperwork finished. Hopefully they need me to start like... yesterday." He laughs at himself. "At this point, I'll start digging through garbage bins on the street for the five-cent recyclable cans."

I peer at the balcony door and jerk my chin up in the same direction. "Better get to it," I tell him. "The street cans are at their fullest this time of the morning." He mocks some laughter and jumps on me, knocking me on my back. I lay on my bed, smiling, as he begins wrapping his hands around my neck.

"Is this really how you want to go out, Keith?" He rolls next to me and we both relax and smile. I look up at the popcorn ceiling and he's looking at me; I can feel his admiration in the air. "Baby, you're so cute. But really! I don't know how to write this email."

I sit up and ask, "Are you trying to butter me up? Give me the damn laptop. Tell me your boss's name."

"Julie," he states. "Don't send it yet!"

I shush him and begin typing:

Hi Julie,

First off, I wanted to thank you for taking me on this year as part of the team. I've had an incredible experience with you making the job quite enjoyable. I look forward to continuing there for the summer and into the next school year. I know we have some time off before the summer semester begins, but I would like to put this on your radar now in order to plan accordingly for all parties involved. I recently had a turn of events with my living situation for the summer and will be bouncing back and forth between Columbus and Cincinnati until I find a permanent residence

in Columbus. With that being said, I am hoping you can
work with my schedule and keep my days consecutive
throughout the week, Monday through Thursday being
most ideal.
If this doesn't work for you, please let me know and I
will do my best to adjust. I would love to work with you
during the summer.

Best Regards,
Toby

I hand back the laptop and Toby reads over my work. "Okay, why did you make it look so easy? I would have rewritten this email a minimum of twelve times." Leaning his legs on the bed between mine, he says, "You're so sexy when you're all business-y and professional."

I shrug with a grin on my face and say, "She's a human, too. She should understand, and if she doesn't, she's not the type of boss you should be working for."

"That's right, bee. I'm glad you know your worth, 'cause I sure don't know mine. Typically, I'm scheduled the morning shift at the library, which works great because I can be night shift at the diner and have the weekends here—with you, where I'd rather be." Still standing, he reaches his hand over my shoulder to scratch my back. I look up to find his teeth gleaming as bright as a glass prism in the sunlight coming through the window. How do I resist his smile?

I reach for Toby's chin to pull his lips closer. Next thing I know, he lays atop me. A kiss from my lips moves to my neck, to my shoulder, and continues down Route 69 from there.

We roll over and embrace each other in silence for a bit. My head is placed in his armpit with his arm around my neck, while he lightly grazes my chest and arm. He stares at the ceiling, softly saying, "I wish you could lie here with me all day."

"Me too, bee." I roll over to check the time. "Oh shit. I have to go." I get ready and grab one more kiss for the road.

* * *

"Look at you, girly. Early as can be!" I exclaim as I see Nellie inch through the front doors of Papa Smurf's. "Don't you just look thrilled to see another day here?"

"You know I hate this place. I can't wait to be famous," she responds as she slaps her backpack on the workspace counter in the back of the store. She continues with no emotion, "You're glowing. Does it feel any different living with your boyfriend? You all are getting serious, aren't you?"

I laugh as I sit on the counter. "The living arrangements are legit temporary. He will be gone most of the week because he doesn't want to overstay at his friends' places in Columbus and I want him here so it works out. He is also mindful of overstaying at my place. But truthfully I don't mind."

"Of course you don't. Are you getting laid every single night or what? Keith!" she exclaims, as if something clicks, "You got laid this morning, didn't you? That's why you're so happy."

"I didn't get laid. We agreed we weren't having the sex for a while. Remember?"

The refresher clicks. "Right, you can't get pregnant if you're celibate. I, too, live by this motto."

Through my laughter, I manage to say, "It's great, and he plans to find a place in Columbus within the next few weeks. We're having no issues. As a matter of fact, my knight in shining... something... awaits at my place. We are going to dinner tonight!"

"A date? I *love* being wined and dined! Where are you going? I'm living vicariously through you tonight—my boyfriend's idea of romance caps out at giving me a kiss between Call of Duty matches." She shakes her head in disappointment. "I have to do something about him. Anyway, I need all the details—ASAP." Nellie's excitement spikes.

"He didn't provide much detail. Look for yourself." I open my phone to show her.

"Hi baby, I just want to thank you for letting me stay with you, so let me take you out tonight. As a small token of my gratitude. Nothing crazy, maybe a movie if you're up for it. I have a special place in mind for some good eats (:"

"You don't need to do that, Toby. But I can't resist a good surprise so you know I won't say no," I respond.

"Umm... yes he does. Don't let him think he doesn't 'cause then he will never appreciate anything you do. Set the standard and set it high, boy," Nellie screams with passion.

"I'm just being nice. You know I love food." I point back at the phone.

Toby's text reads, "Perfect, I didn't think you would. I'll be back to pick you up after I run some errands (:"

"What are you going to wear? Oh, I hate surprises; I don't know how you do it. I need to know where I'm going so I know how hot to look." Nellie worries while tapping her temples.

"Surprises have become our thing. Although, my last surprise didn't go the best. But still," I reminisce out loud.

"Well, you know I can hold down the fort here if you want to go. We both know tonight will be slow as hell, so I brought my computer for the occasion. Netflix, here I come."

She begins to pull out her laptop. I give her a big hug and head home.

* * *

I take in the moment as I ride shotgun through the hilly suburbs of Cincy, almost resembling San Francisco with the architecture of the homes staggering up and down the hills. Toby's hand rests on my thigh while the other grips the steering wheel. Andy Grammer blares through the speakers, overpowering the wind.

The car slows and we pull into a bumpy, hole-filled parking lot. The building favors an old factory, yellow bricks with shattered, boarded windows all around. No signs along the building indicate what it houses, except for the one hanging on a gray door at the top of a flight of crooked concrete steps. "What *is* this place?" I question.

"You'll see. I made a reservation for us," Toby says.

"This reservation doesn't feel right and I'm not sure I would eat anything from this place, bee." I bring out my animal voice, pulling my chin back to project the most nervous tone. "No offense, but I'm kind of scared."

"If I told you they didn't serve food, would you be more open minded here?" He laughs and explains, "It has one of the top ratings in town—five stars actually."

"Five stars on what? Rotten Tomatoes?"

We open the doors to exit the car and cautiously approach the stairs. As I approach the door, I grab the handle while reading the faded, dented metal sign that states, "RESERVATIONS ONLY! PLEASE CALL!"

I look back to Toby, who patiently waits on the step below me with his hand on my back to pace his steps.

"Just go in. He's waiting on us," Toby instructs.

"He?" This feels similar to the start of a murder mystery episode I've seen before. *Oh hell, why not?* I pull the latch open to see yellow-hued lights hang between exposed pipes and structural beams in the ceiling. As my vision adjusts, I begin to see massive canvas laundry bins on wheels side by side, which create aisles. PVC pipe racks hold signs that denote the prices of the food listed on red sheets of paper. I take a few steps toward the aisles and pause, taking it all in. There must be a hundred racks of jackets, pants, and shirts—all color coordinated.

"Hi y'all. Do you have a reservation?" A man in a cowboy hat and a cowhide vest steps into sight from a back office, lit by a measly lamp in the corner and accompanied by a foldable six-foot table, artistically detailed with Sharpie doodles.

"Hey! I'm Toby A. Edmonson; I made a reservation for us to look over your selection."

"Ah yeah, y'all have a look around. Now, the dressin' rooms are over there," he mentions, pointing toward the back corner over the racks. "When y'all are ready, I will be in this here office." He has one hell of an accent. I can't focus on anything else at this moment.

"Thank you so much," Toby says, interrupting my southern gaze.

I grab Toby's arm and say, "This is insane!"

"Pel Vintage—isn't this the one you've been wanting to check out?"

"Yes, how did you get an appointment? You got in so fast. I thought only big wigs could manage this," I ask.

"Well, I may have pulled some strings. Essentially, we spend at least one hundred dollars in thirty minutes or we pay him one hundred dollars for this thirty minutes—and he doesn't get any cheaper. We got extremely lucky, so you have some shopping to do."

"Hold on, we only have thirty minutes?" My jaw falls to the floor. "Bye, don't talk to me. Lots to peruse." I begin walking away, looking back with the biggest grin on my face. I mouth the words "thank you" to him. He blows me a kiss and we start our journey of compiling pieces to try on.

As we cross paths at the back of the store, near the dressing area, Toby asks, "You're enjoying the music, aren't you?"

"The playlist won't quit with the classic masterpieces!" I say while placing my stack of clothes down on a pile of messy curtains and blankets in a broken linen bin.

"I can tell! I hear you singing, or screeching. Not entirely sure which one!" Mildly insulted, I take the hanger from the shirt in my hands, chucking it at him and knocking him on the front side of his shoulder. His high school soccer skills won't allow him to catch the hanger, but he most definitely has another plan.

Toby laughs while approaching me, asking, "Oh yeah? Is that all you got?" Reaching both arms out and placing his foot behind mine, he sends me over the broken arm of the laundry bin, but I grab onto him and pull him in with me. Surprisingly comfortable, we lay in the musky blankets for a few seconds. First I laugh, then smile and admire his sweet face. I reach my hand over and grab his neck, pulling his lips closer.

Sending my hand through his hair, I tell him, "Thank you for setting this up."

"You're welcome baby." He pulls back to avoid my hand, since he fixed his hair prior to coming here. "It would be beneficial if we tried some of these things on, don't you agree?" He winks.

Toby struggles to get up from the blankets. "You can go first," I say as he balances himself.

He reaches his hand out for mine to assist and adds, "I meant concurrently," leading me to the dressing room. While stunned, I don't reject the offer.

* * *

"Gentlemen, your reservation time is 'bout up," Rawhide Vest announces while searching the aisles.

I yank up my shorts and peek out of the blue velvet curtain of the dressing room. I slide out and grab the clothes I acquired earlier.

"We are over here! He's in the dressing room finishing up." There goes my attempt at being slick.

Rawhide looks down at all of Toby's choices in the broken bin. He slowly turns the opposite direction, instructing us to meet him at the front, in the most unamused tone.

Toby slides the janky curtain back and hands over my hat. "You forgot this."

My eyes widen as I admire my curls in the dressing room mirror, equally as janky as the curtain. "Shit. I tried to act normal. How did I do?" I smile and begin to laugh.

"It's fine. I hope you didn't like this place too much. We won't be returning for a while," he says happily as he sorts his plain two shirts he picked out. "I only have about twenty bucks worth of clothes here."

"No worries. I can make up the difference with the stockpile I acquired." Sifting through my stack, I ask, "Will you go start the check-out process so I can buy some time? I'm scared to keep him waiting anymore, as he might uncage the wolves in the back."

I walk up just in time to catch the back end of their conversation, "...Keith. We're dating and I just surprised him with this reservation." Toby waits for a reaction.

Rawhide stalls before saying, "Toby and Keith. You know, he shops here occasionally when in town—Toby Keith." Even Toby Keith seemed unamusing to him.

"Wow, exciting! I told you the big wigs come here," I chime in while laying my items on the counter one by one, reevaluating my choices. Rawhide rings them in as I set them down.

"You're about six bucks short." Rawhide all of a sudden gains some emotion.

I look at Toby. He shrugs and looks at the hat rack. Grabbing a yellow cap with red stitching around the edges, he slaps it on the counter and we get the hell out of there.

Toby and I roll down the concrete steps from laughing so hard what just happened. I fall in the passenger seat once again. "Stop sexin' in my dressin' room and come to the front," Toby mocks in a deep southern voice, nailing Rawhide's demeanor. We ride through the hills, still mocking him.

"Where to next?" I ask in Rawhide tone.

"Just sit back and enjoy the view." Toby points to the window as the city skyscrapers appear over the highway and the sun sets in the back. Exiting toward the beauty's direction, we park close to a familiar park on the water.

Toby reaches for the bag we just acquired, grabs the yellow hat, and replaces the one on my head. I pull down the visor to find a pastel rainbow, front and center. I leave it just where he placed it as we exit the car. His hand tugs mine as we near the park's concrete path through the grass. My little heart floats behind him. We walk the park, stop at a gyro food truck, and throw feta cheese at one another, while watching the sun set in the sweetest little park.

As I sense the evening coming to an end, I grab Toby's hand and say, "Come with me."

"Should I be scared?"

"Potentially. Hopefully the troll isn't home." I lead him under the bridge running over the water. An oval-shaped cave sits tucked away in the stone pillar holding the bridge.

"Whoa, I've never seen this. How do we go in?" Toby questions.

"The gate usually stays closed, but you can squeeze in between these two poles. They're just a bit wider than the rest." I demonstrate.

Toby follows and wraps his arms around my waist as he trips through the gate. "It's chilly in here, isn't it? Peaceful, though. I'm a fan."

We sit with his arm around me in the moist air and listen to the river flow. "I come here and think about life on occasion—when I'm overwhelmed," I explain. He rubs my arm and we lean our backs against the stone as I put my head on his shoulder and embrace the moment.

Just him and I, together.

CH. 13

MY ATTIC

Toby returns to Cincinnati rather late after his first week at the diner. He tiptoes into my room with his arms full of bags and totes, expecting to find me asleep.

"Hey baby, sorry to wake you," he whispers.

I look over as he unloads the bags onto the floor in the corner. "You didn't; I'm just watching some music videos. I missed you. How did work go at the diner? I want to hear all about it."

His laughter evolves into greeting me with a peck on the head. "It's only been four days, bee. But it ultimately went well and I have great news!"

With excitement, an intrigued "ooh" erupts from my mouth, followed by "do tell more," and me sitting up in bed.

"I got to talking with this guy, Mark, from the diner. He and Brock are friends through the fraternity they're in. They actually just voted Mark as president of their fraternity. We were able to talk about how to join and the costs, so he cleared up my questions. Looks like I'll be rushing before the fall semester."

"Nice! If you think it's a good idea, you should." I essentially forgot about my fraternal experience until this moment.

"Does he give you good vibes? Is it expensive?" Rapid fire, I shoot off with the questions.

"Whoa." Toby laughs, overwhelmed. "Since Kevin and Brock are in the same fraternity, the vibes fit considering how much time we spend together. The price isn't exactly cheap but I explained my situation to him." Toby walks over, leaning his thighs on the side of the bed while grabbing my hand, adding, "He has a place for me to live! It would be unbelievably cheap because it isn't actually a room—more of an attic space, from his description—but enough room to be inhabitable. If that's the case, I can save money this summer to get ahead for the semester. It could be good for me to join and make some more friends."

"Well, that's great news! Do you think you should live with this guy, save money this year, and revisit the fraternity idea next year once you're really ahead?" I suggest.

"If the diner continues to be this busy then I will be fine. I made some decent money this week. And I ran it by Kevin last night since he studies accounting and all. The numbers seem to make sense to him."

"Oh nice, is that where you stayed—with Kevin?"

"What? That's really your next question? I didn't have a choice, so yes, I did." He seemed rather annoyed.

"It's just a question, Toby. Sorry, why are you getting so defensive? Truthfully, I'm happy for you! When can you move in?"

"I don't know, I wanted to run it by you." He rummages through his bags, avoiding eye contact with me. "Seems you're all for it, as long as it isn't Kevin or Brock, right?" He finally looks at me.

"No, I definitely have questions about this guy, obviously. But, yes, I'd be happier if you didn't stay with people you've had previous sexual history with. But, I know your situation is…"

He cuts me off, saying, "Okay, I will move in with Mark right now. Can you stop being insecure so we can move on from it? Kevin is not an issue, Keith. Brock is not an issue—point blank," he says, stern as can be while looking at me from across the room. "Shit, seems like you'd want me in a homeless shelter before staying on their couches."

"Toby, really, it's just a question. I'm not concerned about Kevin in the slightest. I didn't mean for you to get upset. I apologized; just calm down and come to bed, please."

"Okay, it's been a long few days. I'm going to brush my teeth. Give me a second."

Damn, why did he get so defensive about that? We've hardly spoken; I just wanted to catch up on how the week panned out. I'll just lie down and let him get some rest. Maybe he'll realize his reaction was uncalled for.

When Toby crawls into bed, I pull him closer. "Tell me more about this Mark guy. What does he go to school for?"

"Well… he's even older than me, by six years, which would make the full college experience even scarier for me."

"Oh, for sure odd. Usually someone his age would take night classes or something."

"I agree! He has a kid, which definitely plays a big part in his delay, but he only has her every other weekend so it's not too much of a problem to combine it with school. If a problem arises from her being there while I am, I could come here or make myself disappear when she's around. I'll be working a lot so it won't matter."

"It's definitely valuable to get the full college experience, if possible. I know I'm thankful for it. How old is his daughter?"

"She's four. And I'm glad I met him because I didn't think I could join a fraternity either, being older. I know my friends have told me otherwise, but I would still feel strange about it. Mark explained how he brings his daughter to events sometimes and the guys love it. He just seemed really enthused and invested in my well-being, so I feel really good about it."

"Having people around that care about you is important, you know? I had a great time in my fraternity for a while. It hasn't really been the same since the last tailgate." I start to reminisce. "Probably a one-off situation, though."

"Right. It'll be fine. He told me I could move my things in whenever I wanted."

"When do you want to get your things over there? Are you going to need my help?"

"I should be able to manage with just my car. I just have to see when Mark would be okay with me starting the process."

Trying my best to lend a hand, I double check, "Are you sure? You know I don't mind helping."

"I promise, it's okay." He follows with a kiss.

* * *

The next Monday, Toby moves some of his stuff in and gets settled. He gives me a tour via FaceTime upon moving in.

"You finished so quickly," I say as he approaches the small, white-vinyl house.

"Yeah, Rory brought my mattress up and helped. Bee, look at the chimney from out here; it's cute and will be so cozy to have." He walks in the white front door to the living room with the fireplace facing the tan couch. Behind the couch is a little walkway that leads to the only technical bedroom. "That's Mark's room." He shows me a glimpse of the master, which is as unkempt as you'd expect from a single dad in college.

Mark lies in bed on his computer while welcoming Toby. "Look at you, roomie," he says as Toby peeks in. I try to get a good look, but all I can see are his long legs and rounded shoulders peering out of his red cut-off shirt.

Toby laughs and continues the tour. "Okay, let's see the kitchen." As he walks through the open space, the cabinets line the back wall. "If you follow around the dining table, you can make it to my attic!" He points to the back corner of the dining room, adjacent to the cabinets, which holds a door leading to a carpeted stairway landing and a rather small bonus room with a small circular window in the top ridge.

"Your attic? Is that what we are calling it now?" His excitement transfers to me as I begin to smile. The camera reveals the room, a rather empty space. Toby's mattress sits on the floor along with a small desk lamp next to it. "Are you excited to be all moved in?" I ask as he plops on his bed.

"Yes, this will make life much easier, until Paul and I land a place when he's back for school."

"Does this mean you're never going to see me again? You're a busy bee these days." I give a side-eyed grin to the phone to emphasize the joke.

"No no, we will make it work. Don't be like that, bee. You make time for the things you want to make time for—and you're one of those things. I hope I am for you, too." His response is reassuring and he seems to have a weight lifted off his shoulders now.

This will be good for him and us. I can already tell.

* * *

"I wish you could have stayed on the phone. I feel uneasy being here alone," Toby texts three days later after we talk on the phone.

"I already miss you, bee. What's creepy about it? You've only been there a couple nights."

"I'm not the biggest fan of the darkness. My door opens sometimes and I feel like eyes are staring at me. When I get to the door, there's no one there, but it still gives me a weird vibe."

"Oh, don't be such a baby. Mark's kid wanted to play a joke on you. Now it's getting to your head."

"Yeah..." He neglects to mention that she hasn't been at the house since he moved in. "I still wish you were here," Toby insists.

"I'd protect you from the four-year-old monster LOL."

"LOL I think she could take you. She's devious."

"Honestly, you're right. I usually stay away from violence," I admit.

"Can I call you?"

"I'm going to sleep as soon as I lie down. I am so tired."

"That's fine, can we sleep together on the phone? Like we used to do in the dorm?" he asks.

"Of course, I'll call you in a bit."

Sleeping on the phone together gives me one of the best feelings. It's a hard feeling to describe but it really gives a sense of presence and makes us both feel needed. On occasion, we can hear the other moving or shuffling and will whisper, "Bee, are you okay?" It's gentle and sweet.

I give him a call and we wish each other good night before heading into our dreams.

* * *

I wake up around four in the morning to the sound of a blanket rubbing against my phone. It's louder than a faint touch, almost as if someone was cleaning the screen with a blanket. I whisper, "baby," to make sure Toby's awake. I hear a sniffle and then the sound cuts off. Silence.

The phone shows time progressing, but with no sound I assume Toby is sleeping and I go back to sleep too.

When I wake up again around nine in the morning, I quickly shoot a text to Toby, checking in on him after the weird sound I heard the night before.

"Good morning :) Is everything okay?" I text.

"Yes, why wouldn't it be? Did you sleep well?"

"So peacefully. I did wake up and thought I heard you sniffle and ruffle the phone around quite a bit."

"Oh yeah, I woke up to go to the bathroom and took you with me (:"

"Ugh. I loved every second of it, unknowingly (:"

"Can we sleep together again tonight?" he asks.

"I want nothing more."

* * *

That night, I wake up randomly around 3:00 a.m. and proceed to check on my boy. Nothing is coming through the phone; I can't even hear the little fan in his room that is usually on in the background. He's obviously muted his phone from his end. Confused, I try not to think about it and go back to sleep.

The next morning when I wake up, I reach out to Toby about him muting his phone.

"Did you put me on mute last night?" I ask via text.

"I woke myself from a bad dream and thought I would be talking in my sleep."

"Oh no. Sorry, baby! Tell me the dream. Did it scare you?"

"Basically, I saw Auntie Amanda getting chased by a car and then getting thrown in. Rory and I were little, just watching from the street with no one to care for us."

"Toby! It's okay, that's a thing of the past. You're fine and independent now (: I'm here, everyone is still around."

"I know, I just didn't want to wake you):"

"You can wake me up whenever you need to, bee."

I don't hear back from Toby until way later that night, just around eight. He texts me his evening plans.

"I'm going to stay at Kevin's tonight. He has some furniture for his living room he needs help putting together. There's glass in some places so he wants to be sure it doesn't break," Toby shares.

"That'll be a fun little project. Would love to see them when they're done," I request.

"I'll be sure to get a picture." But he never ends up sending me one.

The next evening, after my own busy day of work and errands, I realize I never got the photo of the completed furniture and shoot Toby another text.

"I just realized, you never sent me a picture yesterday!):"

"Baby, I forgot to take one! I'll see if Kevin can send one," Toby responds immediately.

"How's the diner tonight?"

"It's good. Going to go home and crash once I get out of here. Can you sleep with me?" he requests again.

"Yes, please. I missed you last night."

* * *

It's around two in the morning this time when some scratchy noises come through the phone from Toby's end, waking me up.

"No, no, no." I can hear Toby sleepily plead, before suddenly, all sound is cut off on his side. He's muted again. I wonder if he's having another nightmare and I worry.

Those dreams are really bad for him.

I wish I was there to help.

CH. 14

534

There are only two weeks until the fall semester starts and I spend the weekend in Columbus. Annie and I lend a helping hand to get Toby moved once again, while also obtaining our first walk-through of the new apartment he will be sharing with Paul.

On the way to his new place, I am following Toby's car when I glance into my rear-view mirror and see the T-Rex stare back at me. I reflect on how far our relationship has come since the beginning of the summer, nearly three months ago.

These last few weeks, I've felt he's been distant but I'm just in my head again. I should make sure he knows how I feel. Otherwise, we have grown so much, together. We spend every second possible with one another. We've become a pair.

As far as Toby goes, individually, he's grown so much on his own. I am proud of him for working so hard. He never really asks for anything. He basically has gotten himself out of this shitty situation all by himself. He has his mind and heart set on a different lifestyle and I can't wait to see him live out his dream.

As we pull into the complex, a white sign flanked by two bushes and nice landscaping welcomes us to the "Glass House Apartments." The entry road dips down a small hill with trees lining the side. At the bottom of the hill lies a white-washed brick leasing office with some parking spaces out front to host guests for the office and the pool.

As we continue, I see three-story buildings on either side of the road lined with white vinyl, gray trim, and balconies paired with each unit. We pull into the opening gap between two buildings, with one of the buildings almost caddy cornered to shape the cul-de-sac, bringing the complex to an end. The gap opens to a parking lot around the back with plenty of spaces available.

We all open our driver-side doors, while Brachi jumps from Toby's lap into the parking lot. "We made it, Toby! How excited are you?" Annie hollers as she comes out of the gate, kneeling to Brachi's level. In a high pitch tone she says, "We know you're happy, baby girl."

With a big smile on his face and his nervous tick manifested in a raised shoulder, Toby says, "I'm so excited! I get my dog and my own bathroom and... yeah. I get my own bathroom. That's 100 percent what I'm most excited about." He looks for our reaction, which says "confused but let's just roll with it and be happy for the kid." He recovers and adds, "Just kidding. There's so much excitement surrounding this."

I laugh, pointing at the stairway and asking, "Do we get the ultimate tour? I did see the pool as we came in. I know where I'll be all semester!"

"Yes, let's go! Can't wait to get in the pool. Which floor are we headed to, might I ask?" Annie's concern is apparent considering the three cars full of boxes.

Toby leads the pack up the stairs and looks back at us with a face already expressing an apology for what he's about to say. "It's on the third floor. We didn't want anyone above us." She lets out a sigh but says, "I understand completely. Just need to mentally prepare myself."

"Annie, yes girl, you get me. Happy to help, just need to let my legs know they're about to start burning," I say as I take the last step. The wooden stairs lead to an open concrete platform on the third floor where the breezeway holds four front doors. We approach the only one missing a doormat in front of the black door.

"534. An amazing number. Let's get in here," Annie says with enthusiasm.

"Yeah... a great number?" I agree, with a confused laugh. "Do you have the key?"

"Paul said he left one around here somewhere." Toby reaches around the door frame but can't manage to reach the top. He looks at me and then back at the top of the door frame. I smirk and step forward, brushing my fingers across the dusty wood and knocking a key to the ground.

"Yep. There she is!" After acquiring the key, he unlocks the door to reveal the bright, white-walled apartment. The tan carpet runs throughout and the apartment seems mostly updated. The unit opens to a small foyer with a coat closet and a doorway to the second bathroom. The bathroom has another door directly through leading to Paul's room, who already has some essentials moved in, such as a couch and a bedroom set that looks rather new.

The space opens to the living room, which holds the couch, perpendicular to the balcony door. The stone fireplace sits caddy cornered between the balcony and Paul's bedroom.

The kitchen connects to the dining area, which sits adjacent to the second bedroom doorway.

Egging on Toby's bathroom obsession, I start hollering, "Look at this bathroom, boy! You are about to get your scrub-a-dub-dub on in here!" Laughing, we all make our way back downstairs.

* * *

Knock, knock, knock. Brachi lets out a few small barks.

"Pizza's here." Annie runs to the door while Toby and I unpack some things in his room—literally and figuratively.

"Baby, what are you feeling?" I ask while setting my box aside to wrap my arms around him from behind, grabbing his chest. "Are you still going to sleep with me every night on the phone?"

"I'm feeling happy to share this moment with you. Thank you for being here, again. You've helped me move too many times... and... I would rather you just be next to me than on the phone." He stands on my toes and rises to give me a kiss while we have a moment of privacy. He looks down and breathes a sigh of relief. "I can already feel the weight lift off my shoulders. I'm already at ease being here."

"Weight from what?" I ask, as if I didn't notice the tension he has been carrying for a while now. "I did want to talk to you about that."

"I moved not even two months ago. At least I know I'll be here for a year. So that's one thing. But you want to talk about what?"

"While you were there, you were distant other than us sleeping on the phone. And even then, it felt like you might be a tad off, or overwhelmed. I know you were working a lot so I just want to make sure it's all in my head and not something I did." I approach with caution.

"Just being at Mark's was—"

"Boys, let's eat!" Annie yells from the other room.

"We can talk about it later. It's not you." Toby grabs my arm and releases it once we exit his doorway. "I can't tell you how pumped I am for this pizza. Thank you all so much for helping!"

"Any activity with pizza involved, you can count me in." Annie opens the pizza boxes on the kitchen counter.

We settle in to stuff our faces. Annie and Toby take the two seats on the couch while I grab the floor, with Brachi watching every move my pizza slice makes. Looking up at them, I grab Annie's attention, asking, "How stoked are you all for school to start back up?"

Annie chimes in, replying, "I genuinely can't wait. I'm taking a class on counseling for kids. One of the topics they discuss is divorced parents and how to handle the trauma kids suffer from it. I think it will be rewarding, so I'm excited to even get a spot on the roster."

"Maybe after this class you'll be able to understand why Keith and I are so messed up." Toby targets our youth.

"Well, now that you mention it, I will need to interview a few folks with separated parents and I planned on asking you, Toby. But Keith, if you would be available and willing, I would love to interview you too. The project usually starts off the semester; it's the first big one we do. At least, that's what people have told me from past courses."

"Of course, Annie. I am an open book these days. It's part of who I am!"

She jumps up a bit, giddy for her project while wiping tomato sauce from her cheek. "I can't wait. This will be great!

I will actually be in Cincinnati in a few weeks, so maybe we can just do it then, if that's okay?"

"Amazing, just let me know. I would love to get lunch or coffee!"

Annie heads out after eating pizza and we say our goodbyes.

While Toby brushes his teeth, I ask him, "Do you want to continue talking about what you mentioned earlier?" I wrap my arms around his chest, looking in the mirror.

"I'm pretty tired." He spits in the sink and gives his mouth a rinse. "Can we just go to sleep?"

"Of course, baby. Are you sure you're okay, though? If you're upset, you can tell me."

"I'm sure." After we crawl into bed, Brachi lays between our legs while Toby gives me a kiss and we settle into the mattress on the floor. "Thank you, again. Sleep tight, bee."

I give him one last squeeze. "Goodnight."

CH. 15

BLURRED LINES

———

A couple weeks pass and Annie reaches out for lunch as promised.

We meet up for pizza today in downtown Cincinnati. Sent with high regards from Annie, I approach an old historic home that has been restored into a restaurant. The house sits as close as it can to its neighbors, two stories shooting straight up to the sky, parallel with the brick homes next to it. The bottom half resembles a normal storefront, with glass windows from the floor to the ceiling and advertising posted along the glass. There are also tables on the sidewalk out front, with decrepit umbrellas attached that resemble the Italian flag. The second story has crusty windows holding the seventh layer of red, green, and white paint to create an Italian essence.

As I enter, Annie's head is deep in her books at a wooden booth near the entrance. She looks up as the sound of the bells jingle against the door and proceeds to get up from the table to come greet me with a huge hug.

"Keith! Hi! How are you today?" she says with all her enthusiasm.

"Can't complain if I wanted to! How are you?"

"I'm so good! Are you enjoying your classes? I love starting a new semester; it's refreshing and exciting for me."

"I can see that. I'm most worried about my economics course though. Everyone gives it bad reviews, which, I would also do at this point—it's quite the challenge so far. We will see how it goes." I laugh away the pain.

"Oh no!" Her face shows so much concern, as if I told her someone in my family died. "I hope it goes well. You just need to put extra time aside for it weekly, even if there isn't a test that week." It's such an Annie thing to say.

"That's a great idea. I'll manage one way or another; I've cruised through some tough classes before. Tell me more about this one. They teach you ways to talk to troubled youth, basically?" I inquire to get to the point.

"Yes, so obviously we don't all have access to younger children with divorced parents to talk to and get their insight, but we can talk to those of our age group. Part of the project is to develop a sense of how youth trauma translates to adult life, given each scenario." Annie is clearly knowledgeable about the subject. "I'm going to record this part, if that's okay. Just tell me a little about your story growing up and when your parents separated; then I can ask questions to get the information I need from there."

"Oh gosh. I guess we'll get right into it."

"We can talk about something else first if you want. Sorry, I get excited!" Annie attempts to cover her tracks.

I laugh in admiration of her enthusiasm. "No, no. What exactly do you need to know for the project?"

"You can share what you feel comfortable with from the back story. Then I will get some raw emotion on the cause of the divorce and how the divorce itself has affected you, and ultimately, how it makes you feel to this day."

I take a deep breath and begin. "Okay, I can do that. Well, most of this occurred after the divorce and is just a huge testament to my mother and her devotion to my brother and me." Annie nods. "My parents divorced when I was in fifth grade, so it happened going into middle school—which is a highly developmental part of life, most would say."

Annie looks at me, invested as ever. Nodding her head, she agrees, "Yes, big time!"

"Throughout that time, my mom worked her ass off because she had to: she's a single mom getting no real financial support. She would work through the night and turn around and take us to school."

"Seeing her work so hard and still being present definitely makes a difference," Annie adds.

"Of course! She had two other jobs where she was able to pick up shifts when needed, so balancing the schedules always seemed nuts but we managed."

"When did this woman have time for herself? I need to meet her." Annie looks around, as if my mom would pop up.

"She didn't at all. It almost takes a crazy person to be as selfless as she was since their separation—and before that, honestly."

"What do you know about the reason for their divorce, if you don't mind me asking?"

I laugh. "I don't mind. Simply put, addiction, infidelity, and neglect. You can't build a foundation for two and expect one person to maintain it."

"Well, that will certainly take a toll on how you view a person. Good for her. I bet she's thriving now that you and your brother are out of the house."

"I hope so. She deserves it. I know she's still financially recovering to this day. I mean, this world doesn't make it easy to come back from things like that. It's been almost ten years. Ten years of her only focus being how to feed these two kids." I look around the restaurant. "Shit. There are probably moms or dads in here starting the same journey. It happens so often."

"What a perspective, Keith! I know being an adult is hard. I don't know how I could ever give up on my kids."

"He didn't give up, but he definitely didn't help in any way—not financially, at least. Mentally, I just wanted a break from the guy—or I wanted my mom to rid herself of him. I didn't want to see him but he kept fighting for his visitation rights. I had seen all I needed to know I no longer needed the repercussions of that lifestyle."

"So, do you talk to your dad now? How did it all pan out?"

"I had minimal contact for years. That changed one Christmas after he paraded his third child around I didn't even know had been born. Years later, he made the same neglectful mistakes with that round of kids and is in the same boat as he was with my brother and me."

"Wow! Twice? Well, you know what? Everyone deserves a second chance. My dad used to say, 'Mistakes can be made by the millions but recovering from them is one in a million.' It seems he pushed to defy the saying though: He always gave the second chance because people deserve it."

"Inspiring. To an extent, that's fair and I agree. You can make so many minor mistakes but you're conscious of the larger mistakes you make."

"Keith, wow! I'm sorry you had to endure all of this." We hold a small moment of silence. "How do you feel about it now?"

"You don't have to feel obligated to apologize—it's become the norm in my life and I'm happy with it. Going this long without a father figure, I realize I don't need it. Family can be who you make it; it doesn't need to always derive from your bloodline." She nods. "The divorce also shifted my mindset to focus on succeeding and being financially stress free. The goal is to repay my mom, eventually—however that may be.

"Right. She's done so much. I guess you'll have to give her the world." She flashes me a big smile. "Maybe this is why you and Toby have become so close. His feelings shifted in the same direction, as far as being a success and wanting to set an example for the kids in his future classroom."

Damn. Or maybe this is why I act so crazy about Brock and Kevin being around so much. Or maybe the reason I'm so paranoid about him being distant lately. I need to reel it in.

Annie adds, "I'm sure this wasn't easy. Thank you for sharing. I didn't know any of this about you."

"Well, it isn't quite the first thing you tell someone when you meet." We both laugh and then Annie proceeds to ask some other questions for the school interview. I answer as best I can, growing more emotional along the way. Finally, I realize I need a break from the heavier topics and change the subject by asking Annie, "How's your weekend in Cincinnati? What's the occasion? Did you already mention why you were down here?"

Annie lets out a laugh with me to turn the mood around. "My sister and her fiancé live here so we are wedding dress shopping this weekend. I wouldn't dream of missing it. She will be the most beautiful bride."

"That is crazy exciting! I can't even think about getting married right now. I don't think either of us would be ready for about twelve more years." Grinning to get a laugh from Annie, her head tilts to the side with as she lowers her dark eyebrows, almost covering her eyelids.

"Either of us?" she asks.

"Yeah, Toby and I."

Annie sits back, drops her jaw open, and widens her eyes. She pushes against the table, seemingly in disbelief. "You and Toby are dating?"

I pause. "He never mentioned it?" As the words flow from my mouth, my stomach churns.

Oh shit, I didn't mean to say that. Did we ever confirm he told anyone else after he had a talk with Brock at laser tag? I just assumed he did. Maybe he didn't even tell Brock. Is Annie saying she didn't know?

"No…" The small word enters one ear and racks my brain like a pinball machine. I cross my arms on the table and look down while rubbing the sides of my chest. "I thought he…" My ears perk and my head perk up to look at her, as I wait for her to finish.

"I thought he was dating Brock."

"He what?" I fully expected her to say she thought he wasn't gay.

"He's been staying with Brock so often, I thought they were giving it a go again. I never really questioned your relationship. I mean, you don't really strike me as gay." My heart sinks, but I keep my composure, feeling utterly defeated at this point.

Brock? Why would he stay with Brock of all people? That's my first thought. Toby knows I would hate that, but I suddenly wonder if that's why he never sent the picture of the table he "built" with Kevin; he was at Brock's. My second thought hits and I realize it *was* Brock leaving his dorm that day before the soccer game. He's never with Kevin. *Mother fu… wait. What else has he lied about?*

"I can't say I'm not caught off guard a little here. This is… I'm rather embarrassed. We've been seeing each other, dating, for almost eight months now." Silence wraps us like a blanket. I know Annie can feel me shutting down. I look at her as the tears pile up behind my eyes, holding back the downpour.

"I'm sorry, Keith." She reaches for my hand across the table as I look up at her. Her eyes begin to gloss over, as if she is going to cry. "You don't deserve to be treated this way. You have been the sweetest soul to me and you better believe he will hear my wrath for hiding you like this... and for putting me in this position."

My head hits my arms on the table and they become a washcloth in a bathtub—soaked. I try to quickly pull myself together. "This is not your fault. Please don't feel bad. Can I ask you something?" I continue to wipe my eyes. She nods and hands me a napkin. "Have they hooked up when they stayed together? I saw him leaving Toby's dorm the day I surprised him with soccer tickets, which was the same day Toby and Kevin wouldn't stop texting about something he wouldn't tell me about... could it have been about Brock?" I look to the ceiling, trying to stop the flow of tears, but to no avail. A movie reel of "Toby's Most Questionable Moments" just flash through my head.

Annie shuts down and it's silent between us for a few moments. Finally, she breaks the silence, saying, "You should probably talk to him about this."

It all makes sense now. Of course he wouldn't have sex with me; he's been fucking busy, or busy fucking, rather. *How could I have been so naive? Idiot. Idiot. Idiot.* I silently berate myself before returning my attention back to Annie. "Well... Annie, thanks for being honest with me, but I'm going to head home." I stand and grab my keys while Annie apologizes again.

I quickly leave and go to sit in my car, but instead of driving off, I lean my head against the steering wheel. Frustration boils over and erupts as I yell and bang my head on the wheel countless times. *I should have seen this coming.* Slamming my hands against the steering wheel, I scream, "You were damn guilty with a straight face!"

I get my temper in order and start driving along the downtown road. Andy Grammer bursts through the speakers as I drive with no destination in mind. My instincts turn down the tunes and dial Nellie.

"Hey boo. What's up?" Thank God she answered.

"Where are you?" I ask without hesitation.

"At the library. Lily and Blair are actually here too. I bumped into them. Are you okay?" I hear Lily and Blair asking the same in the background.

"I'll be there in ten minutes."

"Okay, be careful. Should you be driving? I can come get you."

"I'm okay." I can barely get the words out without losing my composure. There's something about the other person knowing I'm upset that causes me to lose it all over again. My tears blur the roads as I drive. The feeling of angst is through the roof. Luckily, I manage to follow the blurred lines to the library and my dark tunnel vision leads me to the usual second floor corner, avoiding everyone I know.

"There's Keith. What's going on?" Lily questions as she sees me walking head down in their direction. I look up and Nellie stands up to give me an extended hug. She knew.

"Is this about Toby? I will kick his ass. You know I will, Keith," Blair says with her fists balled on the table.

"Yeah, it is. I'm not sure what to do and I didn't know where to go," I say while continuing to use my arms as tissues.

"You came to the right place," Lily affirms. "What happened?"

"It's a lot and I know you're studying; I can go elsewhere." They all assure me I should stay. The semester just started and no urgent work needs to be done. With that, the story flows from the beginning. They all silently listen. "Thinking back on everything, it makes sense. I obsessed over Toby talking to Kevin so much since the soccer game. It just ate at me and made an enemy in my head who wasn't even the problem."

"Who actually is the enemy? He cheated on you?" Nellie nudged in. I tell them about my conversation with Annie.

"Wait, he told you he stayed with Kevin, but in actuality, he has secretly been staying at Brock's *and* he kept you under wraps in front of his friends, but brought you around them the whole time?" Blair summed up the scenario.

"Exactly. Plus, we don't show PDA or know how to act in public as a couple yet, so it isn't like we were all over each other for them to catch on."

"Boy, I swear... Who does that? I see what you're saying but... eight months? Damned if I let a man keep me a secret. My arm wraps around his damn bicep and don't come off. Everyone knows we're together," Nellie says.

Blair grabs Nellie's arm, leans over, and hollers, "Right!" while her head swings around looking up to the sky. Honestly, I need their banter to keep me calm; this is good.

I add, "Not to mention, when we were apart at night, we would sleep with the phone on so we could be present at the beginning. We began staying together so much throughout the summer though, so the phone sleepovers diminished. When he moved in with this guy, Mark, we started sleeping on the phone again. But, that's when I started hearing ruffling noises and he would mute the phone or just hang up sometimes, which never happened at the beginning in the dorms."

"You think he had the other guy over to his house *and* kept you on the phone?" Lily asks.

I put my head on the table and murmur through my arms, "Maybe? I'm such a damn fool." Nellie rubs my back and the touch of foreign hands brush my arms as I lose it again. I pull myself together as Lily and Blair take turns giving me positive reinforcements about not needing this boy and about how he served his purpose in letting me be who I am.

"I know what's about to happen. This can't continue, but what I'm most scared of and sad about is letting go of the security he gives me by always being there. He's been my person for months and we have a rare connection. When will I find it again? I know I don't need a guy to make me happy but he sure has made me happy this year—happier than I have ever been, truthfully. I know it sounds crazy."

Nellie backs off and looks at me, moving her head to make eye contact. "No, you're just scared you won't find this connection again. You will, and it will be better next time." My eyes veer away from hers. "You'll have more experience, more knowledge, more power. You will be you. You won't be the 'watch-me-develop-through-my-biggest-struggle-ever Keith,' but the 'I'm-gay-and-proud-and-not-one-person-can-tell-me-I-should-hide-or-be-hidden-for-any-reason Keith.' We love you now more than ever and so will anyone coming into your life. If they miss their shot, then their vision is impaired, baby. You are a *catch*! And I mean mm-hmm catch. Like seared salmon, not tilapia."

"Damn, girl. Don't make me hungry over here," Blair jokes. "But, by golly, I agree. You shine, every. Single. Day.

My experience here has been so much better for knowing you. This boy can eat dust."

"Can you thank him on your way out for us all? For helping you more than we ever could. I mean we all owe him that, as shitty as this situation is." Lily's optimism strikes. "You'll look back and think you could have done something, but you couldn't, Keith. He's fighting the fight you fought for years until you met him. We've talked about this. *He* gave you the courage. You just weren't the person for him. And that's okay. Maybe Brock can be his, since he's telling all his friends about their rendezvous."

"What do I do now?" I ask softly.

"Do we take a road trip to Columbus so we can tell him to fuck off?" The two girls look at Blair with big smiles. "We can't let you make an incredibly long drive in such an emotional state."

Nellie shrugs and says, "Let me go put my road trip clothes on because this won't cut it."

CH. 16

FLICKERING

"Are you busy?" reads the text I send to Toby, knowing damn well he's at the diner working. Of course, I receive no response. We are gaining ground on the diner as closing time approaches. The girls' voices flow through my ears, lifting my spirits by telling their breakup stories and playing the best heartbreak playlists.

"So, what's your plan?" Lily asks as she realizes how close we are. "We did get in the car somewhat aimlessly." We look at each other and laugh at our spontaneity.

"Do you know what you're going to say?" Nellie chimes in.

"I don't really have a plan. I will just text him and tell him I'm outside and we need to talk. If he can't, then we wait and grab some food." I begin to think out loud. Though, the more I do, the more unprepared I sound, even to myself. "Maybe we should have a better plan. What do you all think?"

Blair turns her head at the crowd between the middle console while keeping her eyes on the road. "What if we go in and get a table in his section, let him come up to us, and we tell him you're out here waiting for him. Then we get the other server to get us some food because I am a hungry girl."

"Or, you can just text him when you get there. I'm sure he will respond to a text telling him you're at his work. No chance he wouldn't." Lily brings a good point to the table.

"We can start there and see what happens," I agree, while thinking this plan came together adventitiously. We have no other option and are on the home stretch.

Agh. What am I going to say?

We pull up and obsess over how absolutely adorable the diner looks. I can see why people would keep this place in business. Big windows line the front of the building. Through the glass, gorgeous antique fixtures sit above each black-and-white-checkered table. The bar stools and booths are lined with a sparkly red glossy material and chrome accents. The bar sits as the focal point of the rectangular-shaped building with a cute vintage sign reading "Burgers Shakes and Fries. 5¢ each" above it. Sheet metal wraps the outside with a roof topping it all off shaped like a small, upside-down "Y."

Searching through the tattered parking lot, I say, "I don't see him through the windows and I don't see his car in the parking lot. I guess we all are going in. Let's eat and wait until he texts back," I suggest as Blair manages to snag a front row parking space.

Through the front door, a little redhead gem greets us, "Have a seat wherever you'd like; I'll be right with you." We head to the open corner booth. Little Red comes short order with four plastic, red Coca Cola cups filled with water. "How are you all tonight?" she asks as she does a double take on my flushed face. Insisting we are okay, she goes on with the specials on the menu for the day—classic diner.

The whole time she's talking, I just hear Toby's voice feed me his lies. I had told him I'd come visit him one of these days, but I didn't quite think it would be under these circumstances. "Do y'all have any questions about the menu?" Little Red asks.

"We have one," Nellie said, wasting no time. "Does Toby work tonight?"

Little Red lets her eyebrows show how hard she has to think about the question. "Oh, honey, I haven't seen him. Are we missing him tonight?" she asks.

"That is a good question. But I'll go out on a limb and say he never had to work tonight." Nellie had a hunch, as did we all.

"I can double check our schedule in the back for you. Are you all good friends of his?"

"Something along those lines," Blair quickly blurts. "We all know him distantly well."

Little Red leaves the table. The moment she's gone, Nellie leans her head down in my direction, asking, "How pissed are you knowing he isn't here?"

I laugh it off, replying, "It only makes sense, right? What's one more lie to add to the tally? He doesn't live far from here so should we go check there or should I just call him?"

"There's no sense in driving around town. You might as well call him. The jig is up at this point;

he's caught in his game," Lily says bluntly.

I take a step outside to give Toby a call. As I pace back and forth in front of the diner, I step on the parking blocks in each space, anxiously waiting for his familiar voice to greet me on the other end of the phone. It never does though, as I hear, "You have reached an automated voice message system..." *Shit.*

I proceed with a voicemail, saying into the phone, "Hey. I'm at the diner. You told me you were working today and I clearly see you lied, again. We need to talk so tell me where you are." I let out a maniacal laugh, adding, "And if you're at Brock's, you can guarantee we are more done than we were in my mind three hours ago. Bye." Swinging the door open, rather aggressively, the girls turn to find my fists balled while letting out a deep breath to keep my cool. I slide into the seat.

"What did he say?" Nellie pries.

"He didn't answer. I left a voicemail, which will get the point across."

* * *

Finishing our meals, the reason we drove here finally decides to respond. Or at least, that's what I think initially.

Bzzz.

I look down to my phone on the table just as it begins to sound. The vibrations stop us all in our tracks. We look at each other, laughing at everyone's indicative reaction. I turn the phone over and place it directly back on the table. "It's my grandma," I say while their eyes feast on the phone screen. "She calls to check in a lot but every conversation feels like I opened the door to three Mormons attempting to change my life."

"Wrong religion, Keith. Your grandma is Christian," Nellie sets the record straight. "When Toby does call, how is this conversation going to go?"

"Yeah. I keep thinking about it but I truly don't know. The fact that he hasn't called yet is flat out infuriating. Good thing you all are here or I would just get angrier by the second. It likely won't go the way I imagined it with all the rage I had this morning though; I'm definitely more at ease now."

"That's a good thing; you are a wild child when you're worked up about something." Blair says. We all take a moment to laugh, which helps ease some of the tension that has built up again. "Annie definitely already called and told him what happened. There's no chance she didn't, right?" Blair gets suspicious.

"Shouldn't he call you if he knew you were upset?" Lily asks.

"You'd think so. What if he straight up ghosts me? Wouldn't that be the icing on the cake?"

"He isn't going to ghost you. Maybe he's just taking the longest nap in the world." Lily's optimism isn't helping at this moment.

Blair shames her, asking, "Who's side are you on here?" Going in circles, we get nothing accomplished with this conversation and shift it to a pop culture topic regarding Kim K and Kanye's breakup, as if this was similar.

Bzzz.

The blanket of silence returns as we all stare down at my phone, reading the name that appears on the screen. I can't hear anything except my own breathing in that moment. As I begin to reach down, everything starts again and my ears are hit with the noise of the diner.

I answer the phone with a soft, annoyed "hello" as I stand and make my way to the parking lot.

"I got your voicemail. I'm on my way to the diner. Are you still there?" Toby frantically asks.

"Still here, yes. Where are you coming from?"

"Kevin's house. I'll be there shortly—five minutes. Don't leave."

"Does that actually mean you're coming from Brock's? Every other time you've said you were at Kevin's you were actually at Brock's." I provoke him to see if he cracks.

"What do you mean? Can we just talk when I get there?"

"Sure."

I pace the parking lot as I wait longer than expected—go figure. He finally pulls in under a flickering parking lot lamp and I walk in his direction. He gets out of the car, going in for a hug as I approach. Without entertaining his notion in the slightest, I walk to the passenger side to avoid the potential of his arms going around me and dissolving my rage.

I sit in the seat, my body facing the dash with no interest in making eye contact. My arms cross in my lap with my feet propped up on the glove compartment. "Where were you actually? You told me you had to work today."

"I told you, I was at Kevin's."

"You've told me this before and lied. What's different now?" I cut him off, saying, "You've ignored me all day and all month, frankly. I don't believe you. Have you talked to Annie today?"

"I haven't. Why? Did you have your meeting? She told me you were," he replies, attempting to steer me away from my anger.

"We did. It's come to my attention that every time you were at Kevin's in the past, it has apparently been Brock's. Not sure if I have them confused or if this is some kind of mind game you frequently play, but we should be done playing. Don't you think?"

"When have I been at Brock's and told you I was at Kevin's?"

"Toby, you have literally never told me you were at Brock's. Not. One. Time. But can you confirm you've stayed at his house while you were living with Mark? More than once?" He pauses and takes a deep breath. "I know the truth. Why don't you admit it? Annie accidentally spilled it to me, so don't be mad at her. You got yourself into this."

"Yes." We sit in silence. His admission is exactly what I wanted to hear, yet this victory settles like defeat. Staring at the light illuminating the dark dashboard of the car, I expect more to come, but he doesn't continue. Tears begin accumulating in my eyes.

"Yes to what?" I finally prompt.

"Yes, I was staying at Brock's," he replies.

"Were you staying in his bed?"

"Yes." Toby shuts down, and I can sense him getting upset or sad.

"Did you cheat on me with him?" Silence ensues. "Just tell me Toby. This is already done. The least you can do is give me the peace of mind to not wonder. I know you had a past. You told me from the start. You also told me I could trust you, but here we are."

"We slept together a couple times but—"

"A relief. A couple times. Thank you for enlightening me." The sarcasm flows.

"It wasn't like that, Keith."

"Please, tell me what it *was* like then. You wouldn't even have sex with *me*. This really puts it into perspective for me. Taking it slow... likely story."

"Keith, please. I don't know how to tell you." I can sense his sadness as he grabs the steering wheel and leans on the center of the wheel, placing his head on the edge.

"Tell me what? You've been dating him, too? Are you into some polyamorous stuff I wasn't aware of?"

"No." He leaves me dry again with a single word answer.

"Listen, if you don't want to talk then I can go."

"I don't want you to go," Toby states.

As I stare through the windshield, I don't say anything. This time, we have a longer silence. I know there are still points I need to bring up.

"This isn't something I can just forgive, Toby."

"I don't know what to say."

"For starters, you can tell me the truth. From the beginning. That would be ideal."

Toby pulls back from the wheel, lets out a deep breath, and turns to me. As I turn my head back to him he begins to speak. "I had to stay there, and I teased his emotions to get him to let me stay there."

I pause in confusion before replying, "What do you mean you *had* to? You teased him in what way?"

"He knew we were dating, from the time you met him. He could tell. That wasn't a problem and he respected our relationship. Brock never lost feelings for me though, so we talked about it and he understood. But... one night, I didn't want to stay at Mark's, so I told him you and I were going through a rough patch and I couldn't be alone. I *had* to go there, for my own self-defense."

I let out a breath. "You had sex... for self-defense? Please tell me how that works. It's been eight months. I would have loved for you to come to me to defend yourself." I stop and look in his direction. "That's real comforting, Toby. Can you just tell me why you cheated on me?"

"I didn't just want to have sex with you, Keith. I want to make love to you. Your willingness to wait shows me you're different—and I like that. It creates more of a connection, like at the vintage shop. With Brock, I just needed somewhere to go and Annie's parents' house wasn't an option, and Kevin doesn't have a couch. My mom disowned me, you know, and

Auntie Amanda isn't an option, and I didn't know what else to do."

"When I agreed to wait, I didn't agree to you fucking all of your friends," I say softly, but I can sense something is off. "You had a house, Toby. But the house wasn't an option. Why?"

"I couldn't."

"You aren't helping me understand." I raise my voice.

"I don't know how to tell you." He lets out a large scream while beating the steering wheel. After a few knocks on the wheel, his head connects with the edge again and he begins to sob. I sit there and watch in pure shock. He's clearly hurting. I reach over, scratching his back in uncertainty. He pulls his back away from my hand, seemingly uninterested in my gesture.

The only sounds in the car are his sniffles and the buzz of the parking lot light. After a few minutes of frustration, he looks over at me and softly says, "I'm sorry. Remember when I stayed at Mark's house and had night terrors?" I nod. "They weren't terrors. The terrors were reality."

My heart sinks. Infinite thoughts run through my head. As I begin to open my mouth to ask, he answers my question: "Mark raped me." He doesn't look to see my reaction, but cries, in ample pain.

My emotions spiral with no way of knowing how to react. "Toby, I—I had no idea. I'm so sorry."

He quickly wipes his nose and says, "Don't apologize. I'm in the wrong. You did ask multiple times. I had the opportunity to tell you and I know you would have done what you could, but that's beside the point. I shouldn't have used Brock to get away from it; I should have just come to you—and if I had, you wouldn't be done with me."

"That's beside the point, Toby. It takes courage to recognize being assaulted and takes even more courage to say it out loud to someone. Did you report it?"

He looks at me, defeated. "I've played this conversation over and over in my head. The cops would write it down and toss it in a file. Women hardly get justice when they're raped. I'm a male, raped by a male. The file would never be seen again."

"There has to be something you can do."

"I can't afford to lose my job here, but it's hard to look or talk to him, or even just be around him—which is why I went to Brock's tonight, to apologize for using him."

"How did he take it?"

"Not great. But, he does want to help with taking action against Mark; he's infuriated with him. He wants to get the owner of the diner involved. I really want to just move past it all. I just got accepted into his fraternity and it's just a mess."

"Why couldn't you tell me? You talked to Brock before me. Don't you think that says something?"

"I didn't intend on telling him. I just broke down while apologizing at his house. I couldn't handle the secret anymore. Brock is my friend and we acted normal around each other until it came time to sleep."

"Seems you have some figuring out to do when it comes to your relationship with him. I'm sorry all this happened to you and I am here for you if you need me. But don't let me stand between you and something your heart is reaching for. If Brock is good for you, embrace it."

Toby jumps to respond, "Brock and I aren't compatible, I promise. I don't want to lose you. You are my best friend."

"Don't try making anymore promises to me. I can't trust what you say. I'm already an overly jealous person because of my past family trauma, and with these lies, I just can't look at you the same. No matter how much I want to."

Toby looks to the floorboard, saying, "You've made up your mind, I see."

"You've helped me learn a lot about myself, relationships, and my needs, but Toby, it's time for you to start learning about yourself too. Find what's best for you and own it."

"I can't help but think you're what's best for me, Keith."

I open the car door. "You weren't thinking about me when you were with Brock—and that has to convey a more meaningful message than what you're thinking."

I stand in the light of the flickering overhead lamp and peer through the window to the black seat, wondering if that was the right thing to do or if I just pushed away the best thing that has ever happened to me.

I feel like shit.

CH. 17

OBLIVIOUS

I get back to the car where the girls are anxiously waiting, wondering whether I should tell them what I've just learned. I know they are going to ask about it. As I pull the door handle, I'm greeted by expectant silence and three pairs of eyes looking directly at me.

"How'd it go?" Blair asks once I settle back in my place in the backseat. I let my body become small, placing my elbows on my legs while leaning my head on the back of Lily's passenger seat. I answer her with tears.

It went terribly.

"Keith?" Lily sounds concerned.

My face begins to burn as my blood boils, though this time I'm angry at myself. I continually wipe tears from my face as I look down at the floorboard, unable to put thoughts into actual words. *I could have stopped this. How did I miss it? This is all my fault.*

When I continue to silently cry, no ones says anything, and we all sit there like that for a few minutes. Finally, I break the silence while wiping my nose. "Is my food up there?" I ask.

"Are you kidding me? We are worried sick and *that's* your first statement?" Nellie goes mom mode on me.

With a smile on her face, Lily replies, "Yeah, wait a minute... what's even going on back there in your head?"

"I don't think you're ready to hear it," I preface.

Blair slings her head in my direction, reassuring me, "Baby, we are more than ready for this tea. I think it's time for..."

"The story of the week!" Lily finishes.

I point to the road to make sure her attention focuses where it needs to. Not knowing where to begin, I let it all out. "He was seeing Brock and they were having sex. Many times."

"That little shit," Lily blurts out.

"Right." I let out a deep breath, continuing, "I'm not sure I should be the one to tell you this but I don't think you'll be seeing him anytime soon."

"Right, continue." Nellie rushes me along while anxiously awaiting the latter half of the story.

"I told you all that he would call me at night and we would sleep on the phone together like we did when we first started dating, didn't I?"

"Wait, that's cute as shit. You never told me that." Blair mentions.

"It is, in theory. Then things got weird: He would mute me in the middle of the night, hang up, or I would hear ruffling through the phone—excessive adjusting or something. I would confront him, but he told me he would have night terrors, which caused all of that. Turns out his roommate was taking advantage—assaulting him." My voice cracks a bit. "It was Mark, the guy he lived and works with, and is now in a fraternity with."

Nellie grabs my arm in shock, uttering, "No! He was... raping him? The whole time?"

"With you on the phone?" Lily adds.

"Yes! But there's more." Nellie begins to signal me along. "Toby manipulated Brock by feeding him lies with intent to sleep in his bed to avoid staying at Mark's."

"I mean, is that the worst thing?" Blair questions. "I've led on my fair share of boys to get what I want."

Nellie steps in, adding, "Um... not when you have a *boyfriend* who can help you." I nod my head. "So where did he come from earlier?"

I laugh. "Funny story. He was with.... drum roll, please."

"Brock." They respond in unison.

I give the most exaggerated head nod and Blair whips her head around. "Okay, no. If that boy still likes him, then he needs to figure it out for himself. You do *not* look to the person you are moving on from to help you through all of your mental struggles. I don't care what kind of friends they are. Brock is a damn fool. He's just trouble."

"I agree. Supposedly, he went there tonight to tell him what Mark has done and how Toby used him." My aggression starts to show in my hand gestures. "Before he told *me*," smacking my chest, "what Mark had been doing! Like... should I feel remorseful for breaking up with him? Did I do the right thing?"

Nellie claps between each word, "You. Are. So. Right." She pauses. We all do. "He's been through a lot, yes. I mean this boy was sent through the wringer. Think about it. If his parents weren't homophobic, none of us would be in this car right now and he would have never been raped, let's be real. But, he straight up lied to your face on so many occasions. He messed up! He could have taken so many different paths that also could have avoided hurting you, Keith."

We all nod, in unfortunate agreement. Lily chimes in, "When you're in a relationship, you have to take the other person's feelings into consideration with everything you do, really. He lied. He cheated. He didn't have to do either of those things. He could have come to you."

I look at the floor of the car again. "You're right. I did break up with him. Just seems like he needs me now more than ever."

"But does he *actually* need you?" Lily asks again.

I think for a second. "I think that's part of why I'm so sad. He hasn't needed me this whole time. The thought of Brock has danced around in his mind since before Mark came about, so the breakup has nothing to really do with that, right? This just happens to be how I found out—about *all* of it."

"It's an unfortunate situation," Blair says with a sigh. "But hey, you've said this to me and I'm going to remind you, neither of you know what a relationship looks like or how to have one. The only thing you can do at this moment is learn from it and take it into your next one."

I let out a huge breath. Nellie scoots closer in the back seat and leans her head on my shoulder while scratching my back. "It's going to be okay," she says. "It can only go up from here. For both of you."

* * *

It's almost midnight by the time we pull up to the library back at our school. This day has proven to be far more emotionally heavy than anticipated and I'm exhausted. It also sucks that it's Sunday and I have a full week ahead of me.

"Thank you all for doing this with me. I don't know what this night would have been like without you. You truly are the best," I tell them.

"Keith, we wouldn't have wanted to be anywhere else," Nellie says.

Lily chimes in, adding, "Sorry you had to endure this mess. You deserve the world and it's coming your way."

"I was along for the ride, so don't look at me." Blair doesn't do emotion very well, but she has so much poise and we love her for that.

We exit the car and say our goodbyes to one another. Nellie and I walk away in the same direction when she says, "If you need anything, you can call me any time. You know that?"

"I know. I really do appreciate you more than you know. Can we hang out soon? I'll have people over and hopefully they'll love me again after hardly seeing me for eight months," I exaggerate.

"No one hates you." She laughs. "But yes, I'm sure everyone would love that." She gives me a long hug before she also parts ways with me.

I really do have the best friends—the best support system—I could ask for.

CH. 18

WHITE BOX

—

That Saturday morning, I wake up and promptly text a group of friends a reminder. "I cannot wait to see all of your faces tonight at my place. I'm thinking 7:00 p.m. Bring your A game... I'm going to kick some ass in beer pong!"

Realizing what today is, I send another text: "Hi Mom! Happy Birthday. Have fun at the bachelorette party tonight. I love you (:" Mom doesn't drink, but she's seemingly stoked her birthday falls on the same day as her friend's bachelorette party, which will be downtown near my apartment.

I've missed most of my classes this week from not having the mental or emotional strength to get out of bed, but today I feel a different energy. Making my way to the kitchen, I find my roommate cooking breakfast. "Whats up, my guy? How ya feelin'?" He knows I've been going through some struggles or clearly has suspicions.

"I feel good." I gaze at Drew and instantly realize, *I'm a hypocrite.* I openly ask, "It's no secret at this point... what do you know about my situation? I can fill you in." I'm feeling rather courageous this morning.

Drew gives me a look before responding, "Man, all I was told is you are dating some dude. Where has he been? I haven't seen him."

"Toby and I broke up. We were dating, and yes, I'm gay. I should have told you and this is a big reason why we broke up."

"Because you never told me? Dude, I am an open book. You can tell me whatever you need. Also, Blair may have mentioned it to me."

"No, not because of you specifically. It's an abundance of things, but it starts with not having the luxury of being who we are around the people we surround ourselves with. I haven't been fully myself here, so I want to change that. Anyway, the breakup resulted from his neglect to tell the people in his life who he is and who I am, among... other things," I explain.

"Whoa, wait, she didn't mention all of this. I'm sorry you two broke up." We sit in silence for a while before he continues, "I thought y'all might be dating, but not until Blair told me." He then said something that sticks with me: "Why do you need to label it? And who cares who you bone; it doesn't affect anyone else." We ventured to our shitty little apartment balcony and talked more about when it all started. Drew asks me more normal curiosity questions as well.

Drew is incredibly knowledgeable about life, which leads him to ask, "Do you think you gave him more of a push to come out when he wasn't ready?"

I sigh, reflecting on what he just asked me. "I guess, unintentionally. He made it seem like he wanted to. If he had communicated that to me, things would have been different."

Drew nods his head, adding, "It's crazy how we look at people so differently after they make mistakes. As if we never trusted them or spent eight months with them in your case."

"As unfortunate as it is, I can't put myself through that again." The sound of birds chirping fills the silence that follows this statement. I begin to change the subject. "Speaking of eight months, I've been a really bad friend. Are you up for having some friends over tonight?"

Drew stands up and heads to his room from the balcony. "Yeah, man. I won't be here tonight so it's all yours. Thank you for telling me. I know it's been a rough patch, but you can always talk to me." The birds and I stay motionless to soak in the triumphant moment.

* * *

As my best pals get to the top of the circular stairs from the apartment foyer, I open the door only to get smacked in the face by a familiarly awful smell that congregates in the foyer. Ignoring the stench, I greet them with a big hug and drink in my hand. "Long time, no see. Grab a drink from the kitchen if you're ready to get rowdy."

Nellie leads the pack through the living space, passing the dining room ping pong table. "Anything to get away from this stanky ass old spaghetti smell," she says.

Lily laughs as they reach the kitchen, explaining, "Shit, that spaghetti has been hot boxed inside the car in the summer heat. It's just... bad."

"Who ate such a monstrosity of a meal?" Blair asks.

The crowd trickles in as the beer pong ensues, music blasts through the speakers, and the drinks flow. Holding up a bottle of rum and some Solo shot glasses, I yell over the music, "Who needs a shot? I sure do." Receiving mixed responses, I line the shots up along the kitchen counter and aimlessly pour before distributing as many as I can; there are ample shots left.

As Nellie rounds the corner into the kitchen, she grabs the door frame to support her swing in my direction. She asks, "Should we team up for the next game?" She looks at the counter. "Whoa, that's a lot of alcohol, sir."

"Someone will drink them." I hand her one. "Probably me. Cheers."

With a three-game winning streak, I blatantly sneak back into the kitchen after each win for a celebratory shot... or two. I need them to forget about my demise with Toby. After our inevitable loss, Nellie's eyes get rather wide after following me to the kitchen this time. "Where did all those shots go, Keith?"

"They're right here," I reply, pointing at three shots on the counter. I pick up the bottle and see only four or five shots remain, if that. My eyes widen as I admit, "Oops, I basically drank all of this."

"Um... yeah, everyone has had like two beers, Keith. Lily, Blair, Nolan, and I are the only ones who took one of these with you."

"It really seemed like I gave out more." I'm not too drunk, yet, but I play it off knowing damn well I took the shots. "Oh well. I'm just happy to see everyone." We throw back another shot and head back to the beer pong table.

Noticing my stumbling, Nolan pulls me aside. "Let's catch up, buddy." He and I make our way through the back hall to my bedroom and out to the patio for some fresh air. "How are you? What's going on with you and Toby?"

"We are done and over with." Nolan nods as if he already knew. "I have pushed you all away and I don't want you or anyone else to feel neglected. I love all my friends and I'm sorry I've been so distant." My words begin to slur.

"Buddy, no need to apologize; you know I am always here. I know Lily and Blair would say the same. Hell, so would everyone in that room. Where did you draw the line with him?"

I look at Nolan, then start to tear up. My head shifts upward to the rotted wood above me in hopes it would stop the tears. "It's difficult to form love around an idea of what a relationship should be. We are both young and new to people being aware of our sexuality. I still feel weird saying 'I'm gay' in front of you, you know? And for the same reason, there have been many things Toby wasn't fully honest about. We are all still learning how to be comfortable in our skin."

"Of course, it takes real strength to overcome the things you both have. I'm proud of your journey, man. You're doing great—well maybe slow down on the rum and you'll be doing great."

We share a laugh, "Ultimately, Toby had past relations with his friend, Brock, and continuously lied to me about it. He lied about being at Mark's and at Kevin's, when he actually was with Brock on multiple occasions." Nolan reaches over, grabbing my shoulder for comfort as I crank my drunken tears up a notch. "He cheated on me more than once, but he essentially calls it self-defense sex."

Nolan gains a look of confusion, asking, "What does that even mean?"

"Ugh. This is the hard part."

"We don't have to talk about it."

"It's okay." I look back up to the rotted wood and begin sobbing. I slam my head into my hands as Nolan reaches back over to my shoulder.

"Keith, what happened?"

"His most recent roommate took advantage of him every night. I confronted Toby about being with Brock so much and he said he couldn't stay at Mark's anymore." I perk up and wipe my tears away. "He slept with Brock to get away from being raped."

"Oh buddy!" Nolan says in shock. "Definitely a tough position to be in, but at the end of the day you have to do what's best for you." He pats my back. "This is the right thing to do." He stops to think for a moment. "Maybe he lied about his location so he could avoid telling you about being raped. Maybe he wasn't ready to tell anyone. Regardless, he has others around him who can comfort him and take care of his situation with Mark. This was out of your control, so don't blame yourself for any of this."

Trying not to get upset all over again, I confidently state, "I've wasted enough time on this boy!" I pull my head up, screaming, "Fuck you, Toby!" I see a smile form on Nolan's face, approving my outburst.

I turn around with the intention of going back inside to the party, when I notice the door was closed behind us. When I pull on the doorknob, the door doesn't budge and I realize that it's stuck, the wooden frame swollen from the heat wave. The door has glass panels, some of them cracked, and I peer through one, trying to decide the next best course of action. I decide the best thing to do is just push the door open, since I can tell it's not closed all the way, just stuck.

Just needs a push, my drunken mind repeats.

I begin to reach toward the panels, aiming for each hand to apply pressure to two separate panels, but my emotion and drunkenness give me an adrenaline rush, which exaggerates the force I use to push the door. The moment I make contact with the glass, there's a huge crash and my arms soar straight through some glass panels.

Well shit.

* * *

Next thing I know, I'm leaning over the porcelain sink in my bathroom, which is covered in blood and water. With the water running, I vomit into the sink over the diluted blood before I hear Nellie say, "Y'all, I'm going to call an ambulance," from behind me.

I somehow sober up and snap out of everything. I yell, "No, call my mom!" I look around and see Lily by my side with a wet rag around my wrist. I look to my other side and find Nolan holding a wet rag around my right arm.

"Everything is going to be okay," I say and nod, despite the tears racing from my eyes and the worrisome look on my face.

"Hi Miss Sandra, it's Nellie...," her voice fades as she walks into the other room. My friends surround me in the packed bathroom. Nellie comes back pretty quickly, just as I remove the wet rag on my right arm to find a flap of skin hanging down, exposing something white. "Is that a bone or tissue?"

Quickly replacing the cover, I look to Lily for answers. "Keith, just breathe. You just need some stitches. Your mom is on the way. Right, Nellie?"

"Yes, she's around the corner and leaving the bachelorette party now."

My drunken concerns begin. "She's leaving the party for me? I'm the worst. She never gets to go out." The emotional state ensues as tears begin to form again. I go on, "She's worked so hard and I just ruined her birthday."

Nellie interjects, "Listen, she isn't mad. Just keep your mind off it. Umm... do you all know 'Keep Your Head Up' by Andy Grammer?"

Thinking she's directing her question at me, I croak, "I love that man." More vomit erupts into the sink while everyone around me nods and crinkles their noses.

Within moments, the room fills with beautiful lyrics and my mind begins to calm as I wait patiently over the sink, watching the blood drips come to a halt.

The room grows silent and eerie, while any good thoughts I have disappear. I turn my head to see Sandra turning the corner with a friend accompanying her. With no time to waste or process how fast she arrived, I quickly confess, "Mom! Toby and I were boyfriends! I'm gay and we broke up and I invited everyone over to drink and I..."

The tears begin again, and my mom turns and whispers a few words to her friend, whom I can't see at this point. I still attempt to tell my story, but the crying overpowers any words I attempt to project. Mom slides between everyone in the bathroom while telling me not to cry, shushing me as she reaches for my back. The room clears out, except for Nolan, who gives Mom a rundown of what happened with the door.

"Let me see." Mom pulls the rags off. She scrunches her nose and pulls her head away. "You'll just need some stitches, so let's just go to the hospital. My car is downstairs waiting." Mom mode calmly takes over with absolutely no acknowledgment of the bomb I just laid on her.

* * *

Mom's friend drops us off at the car port of the emergency room. The vibrant lighting and the emergency room sign create a red glow around the port. We walk into a freshly remodeled waiting room. The red rags are still wrapped around both my arms as we enter. I take a seat in a chair next to a side table in the middle of the room and put my head between my knees again. Mom goes through the check-in process while Nellie walks through the door and finds me waiting.

Nellie questions, "What did they say? How long until they can bring you back?"

"Mom is up there checking us in," I reply.

Mom calls me over soon after. Nellie remains in the chair while I am summoned to a strange cubicle in the corner of the waiting room. The walls are about half the height of the room, with gray carpet covering the bottom half and some scratched windows occupying the top half of the wall. I round the entry door of the cubicle and find a dashing-looking man in a rolling chair, facing two stand-alone chairs where he directs me to sit. His green eyes look at me while he says, "Hey Keith; I'm Harry, one of the nurses here. We are going to take some vitals and take a look at what's going on here. Do you want to run me through what happened?" I admit, all I can see is his gorgeous, beard-covered jawline moving up and down.

Talking slowly, I explain, "Oh yeah... so basically I pushed through... a window panel to my patio door... completely on accident. The door was open... just caught at the bottom corner," I mention, trying to play it cool. "I just needed to push it open a little so it stopped sticking at the corner."

"Were you alone?" Mom shakes her head with disappointment before I can respond.

"No, I had some friends over," I add.

"Was alcohol involved?" he asks as he places his strong hand on my heart with his stethoscope up to his ears. "It's okay, no trouble can come from disclosing information here. You're protected through HIPAA laws."

I nod and go on, "I had more than three-quarters of a bottle of Malibu. We had quite the night, or I did, at least."

Mom rolls her eyes and softly questions, "How long do you think until they can get us back?"

Harry unwraps one of my wrists and takes a look, after which he says, "You managed to stop most of the bleeding with the rags and pressure, so that's good news. We have a high volume of patients who need immediate responses and all of our rooms are currently full. I will do my best to get you a room as soon as possible, but right now the wait time is quoted at four hours and forty minutes." It's already past midnight and Mom's eyes widen, looking at me in disbelief. "You're welcome to head back into the waiting room. I would call around and see if another emergency room has a shorter wait."

"I'll hang out here with Harry," I say with a bit of liquid courage and a smile on my face. I've only been openly gay to my mom for an hour and I'm already flirting with a guy in front of her.

Mom seems to have other plans, as she wraps her hand around the upper half of my arm to drag me out of the chair. "Come on, Keith," she says.

* * *

I'm in the process of gossiping with Nellie about Harry back in the waiting room. "He's so hot and put his hand on my ba..." But I stop as I look up at the entrance of the emergency room to find one hot mama walking up to us in an all-white dress. My eyes become as wide as the Nile when I notice Mom's friend from earlier with her, holding a white box. I peer over at mom to find her nodding as if she knew the bride to be would come to the hospital on her special night.

The white box takes its place on the side table by my middle-aisle chair. I apologize and make an attempt at a hug, but retreat right away, realizing "Wait, I don't want to get blood on you!" I look down for the first time, realizing the blood on my white T-shirt and the dark spots on my red shorts. We settle on bumping elbows and I ask, "How was your night?"

"Tonight was incredible, Keith! We had a ball and this has only made it so much more special."

Nellie and I laugh after which she claps back with, "Yeah right, who wants to spend their bachelorette night at the hospital?"

"It's not so much the place as it is the occasion. Ironically, your mom made this cake for me but I felt it was more appropriate here." I look at my mom for a hint of what the hell this lady means.

"The occasion being... me wrecking my arms and being unable to pick up a pencil for two months?" I ask.

Nellie, being the theatrical, dramatic star she is, pulls the white box closer to her and screeches upon opening it. Heads from all directions look at us.

"What is it?" I ask.

Nellie yells, "It's a penis!"

"A penis? For... oh my gosh!"

My mom and her friends crack up. The other patients in the room are all confused but smile at the reactions and sense of positivity in the room. The bachelorette chimes in, "Your mom texted me and told me what you told her tonight after she left the bar." She continues explaining, "I've been married once before, baby. It took me a long time to discover who I am. This is a huge moment, and I am so proud of you for becoming you." My eyes are locked on the blue-and-pink-swirled, fondant-covered penis as I stand next to her.

I lay my head on her shoulder as a few tears roll down my cheek. "This cake is for you, honey."

Nellie's eyes gloss over. I pull my head up and gaze at the bride, telling her, "Thank you. You didn't have to do this, especially not tonight."

"Yes I did. As I said, I've done this whole bachelorette thing before. We went out to get the attention." She gives me a nudge while raising her voice, asking, "What kind of fine dining is this? Can we get some plates?" The laughs pour in from the wounded souls around us. I take my seat next to Mom as I become dizzy. She turns to me and wraps both her arms around me, as I lean my head against hers. Emotional moments don't come often for us, so we soak it in until Mom's friend comes over with some plates.

"Truthfully, I forgot about the cake being in the car. I was instructed to bring it in with me downtown, but no one asked about it. I guess I just forgot about the *hard* work I put into it." The bride kicks Mom's leg as they laugh at her joke. "We were texting about the irony of you getting injured on the day of the bachelorette party, and she suggested we bring the cake here after I mentioned what you told me," Mom says, avoiding all emotion.

"It's 2:00 a.m., so the bars are closed anyway. All the pictures were taken and I wore all the white I needed. We are so done with this party. Luckily your mom is a sober chick so she could come to your rescue, our little damsel in distress!" she says as she reaches to pinch my cheek.

"How did you get here, Nellie?" my mom asks.

"Oh yeah, I had someone from work drop me off."

"You don't have to stay here," I say. "Thank you for coming, I'm sorry I messed up the night."

"I'm gonna stay and have some of this penis cake—that's for certain! It looks so good, Sandra!" Mom smiles and receives more compliments from her friends as they begin to chatter. Nellie shifts her focus back to our conversation, reassuring me, "You didn't mess anything up. Not sure if you could tell or remember, but you were the only one in the party mood. Also, I am just really proud of you for telling your mom. Maybe not the best time or place, but hey, doesn't it feel good? I'll never forget when you told me and I'm absolutely positive she won't forget this."

"It does feel good, but I'm not sure what to say. She hasn't said anything about it."

"This whole scenario speaks for itself," she says, cutting into the cake. "She always has her own way of letting you know she is proud of you." Nellie couldn't have been more right.

We share the cake wealth around the room and leave the rest for the hospital staff. This cake is no joke—it's huge. Not too long after, Nellie scores a ride with my mom's friends and they all head out at around 3:00 a.m.

While we wait another thirty minutes, I reiterate the story to her without the details of Toby—just the physical motion of pushing through the balcony. Afterward, we sit in silence, exhausted. While I finally take another look at the wounds for myself, a nurse announces a name I can't understand, to no reactions from the waiting room. I turn around to the door and notice the dark curls on the nurse's head as she says "Keith!" one more time.

Mom and I make our way to her. The nurse begins to ask, "How are you doing? I know you could be better, but given the scenario, are you okay?"

"I'm fine. I still have my hands, so that's a plus."

My morbid joke lands and she laughs. Mom isn't so entertained though. Realizing mom's sour reaction, the nurse replies, "Oh I've heard it all. Now, we are going to get you in a bed we have available. There is no room available at the moment but there should be a couple coming soon, which we will sanitize and move you into as soon as it's ready. So, you cut your wrists? How'd you do that?"

I explain the accident as she settles me into a crunchy, white bed with the lightest sheet, hardly thick enough to warm an ice cube. Upon finishing my story once again, she leaves us in the random hallway while Mom waits at the end of the bed by my legs.

"Mom," I say in the softest, most vulnerable tone, "Did you know?"

"Well, after you brought Toby around, I had questioned it, but didn't want to make any assumptions until you told me."

I immediately follow up with, "What is Grandma going to say?"

"Keith!" Mom looks at me and grabs my leg, sending a wave of chills up my body. I begin to tear up looking at her. "If your grandma has a problem with who you are, then she has some problems of her own she needs to figure out."

I say nothing while looking down at her hands on my legs.

Around the same time I pull myself together again, Harry walks up and asks, "Are you okay, bud?"

"Mr. Harry!" He starts to pull me along the hallway away from my mom, who follows. "I'm more than okay; just an emotional night." I smile and look at my mom.

"Let's get you fixed up and make it all a little better. I hear y'all brought us some cake."

"Yes, Mom made it! Have you tried it?"

"Not quite," he replies as we roll into a room. "I will be able to, hopefully, after I'm done here." Harry does his thing and starts hooking me up to some wires and other hospital equipment. "So does the shape of the cake associate with the emotional night we've had?"

Laughing a bit, I reply, "It does." With that, I begin to tell him what happened again.

He stops me in the middle as I try to explain the shitty windows on my patio door. "What part of town are you in?"

"Downtown here, across from the high school."

Harry spits out the address of my building. "Is that your address?"

Still a bit drunk, I reply, "Harry, you creep! How would you know?" I didn't even consider the possibility he had access to all my information.

"I live in the same building. Second floor with the front patio."

"No chance!" I sit straight up in the bed and turn my head to make eye contact. "I have never seen you there! I also don't take note of everyone in the building so maybe that's why."

"I also work in the emergency room and have a crazy schedule. Nonetheless, I know exactly the door and type of glass you pushed through. The windows on my balcony are partially held together with duct tape because the landlord won't fix them." This gave my mom some reassurance. "Anyway, continue your story. That's so crazy we live in the same building."

Harry hangs around with some other nurses and doctors, though I couldn't tell who they are. My focus stays on Harry as I tell my story. They chime in with all these medical terms as I talk, like "apply the numbing ointment" and "only the left wrist will need stitches"—important things, I'm sure. Mom sits back in a chair across the room patiently waiting for them to do their jobs.

By the time I've told Harry about Toby, Toby's family, Brock, Mark, and the phone calls at night, he knows just about everything and can't believe what he's heard. The other nurse helping me interrupts before I finish though, advising, "You'll want to leave the bandages on for a few days initially without getting them wet. Change the gauze regularly while applying your ointment to the stitches." I nod my head and Harry grabs my attention again.

"Wow, man. What a story. It's a good thing you have good people around you. I know some moms who wouldn't sit in this room as long as she has, that's for sure." Mom laughs and looks at me so she knows I understand how great of a mom I have. "We're done here, though. You all are good to leave." The nurses help me out of the bed. "I'll hopefully see you around." Harry waves. I smile and hope so too.

Mom drops me off at my apartment and gives me a big hug with an "I love you" attached.

"I love you too, mom." I play it off well and begin to head toward my building. I'm halfway there when I turn around with a big smile and shout, "Happy birthday!" As I continue walking, I look to my right and see Harry's apartment windows, dark as can be except for a string of white Christmas lights drooping in the window. "Thank you too, Harry. See you soon, hopefully."

* * *

A month goes by and I'm briskly walking back to my apartment from class when I hear, "Hey buddy, how's that arm?"

I look up to see these skin-tight blue scrubs on a tall, dark, and handsome man. "Harry! It's good. I have been following the doctor's orders to a T. They weren't able to take the stitches out just yet though."

"Man, it was a pretty nasty cut. I hope the landlord at least fixed your windows afterward." Harry laughs—what an adorable, little laugh he has—while flashing his perfect teeth. "How are things with the boy?"

"I haven't really spoken to him since the day before the incident. He doesn't even know I had a visit to the hospital. I guess that's a sure sign he wasn't the one for me."

"You got that right. After being together for so long, just seems like you would have some contact. Have you heard anything about him and the guy who was taking advantage of him?" He had a great memory.

"One of his friends actually reached out to me recently. She apologized about her accidental spilling of the beans and everything spiraling out of control. Obviously, it's not her fault, but she did manage to tell me Toby reported the president, who then got expelled from the university because of the allegations, until they can further investigate. I'm happy the university is taking it seriously."

"Yeah, that's good to hear in this day and age. Sorry to hear you all couldn't manage to work things out, but there's a whole world out there for you." He begins to walk away, but projects his voice louder as he says, "Hell, you're gonna have that scar longer than you'll have the memories of this boy."

I smile, knowing he's right. There's a whole world out there I'm no longer scared to exist in.

I am who I am, with so much to offer those around me. Toby may not be the one for me, but he has shown me how ugly people can be, how pure people can be, and how "me" I can be.

I'll be forever grateful for that.

ACKNOWLEDGMENTS

Inherently, this story will always be sentimental to me. I am forever indebted to those who have been present and supported me through this monumental journey. With confidence, I know each and every one of you will take the kindness you've shown me and shower the next generation with the same love—welcoming them to be themselves. We all have problems of our own. Be the person you needed in your darkest moments for others in their time of need.

Aaliyah Churchill

Aaron Fegenbush

Adam Spivey

Alexis Vines

Allie Decker

Allison Eaton

Allison Fisher

Allison Kujawa

Allyson Cissell

Annie Matsui

Angela Gallinari

Ann Brumleve

Anna Watts

April Deasy

April Ford

Arianna Young

Ashleigh Davidson

Ashley Ennis

Ayesha Singh

Becky Heil

Ben Zoeller

Bergen Dougher

Beth McMahon

Brianna VanOsdol

Brigid McGee
Caley Bailey
Callie Gray
Caroline Davis
Casey Talley
Cathleen Samples
Chabeli Araujo
Chad Moore
Chester Delph
Colin Keegan
Colleen McManus
Connor McCullum
Connor Toles
David Bean
David Doolittle
Destiney Calvert
Drake Wilborn
Elizabeth Brumleve
Ella Mason
Elle Lichte
Ellie Marsh
Emily Cox
Emily Dike
Emily Hale
Emily Weisenbarger
Erin Spencer
Ethan Crews
Fabian Silvas
Frank Soto
Grace Seekins
Hailey Duff
Haley Banks

Hayley Pack
Hogan Polotnik
Jalen Clemmons
Janice Martin
Jenifer Igoe
Jenna Numann
Jermaine Edwards
Jihad Gatohagire
Jill Karcher
John Donehey
John Harrison
Jonathan Phillips
Joseph McDermott
KJ Olsen
Karen L Gross
Kathleen M Williams
Kathryn Nowak
Katie Jones
Katie Tilton
Kayla Derousseau
Kayla Elias
Kayla McMahon
Kelsey O'Bryan
Kim Wagner
Kinley Kaelin
Krystalanne Brunelle
Kyle Kocinski
Landon Matney
Laura Peavley
Madeline Doolittle
Madeline Paganetto
Madison Knies

Madison Mulhall
Makayla Claussen
Mariel Swann
Mark Bushy
Mark Newcomb
Mary Crocker
Mason Wills
Matt Pennington
Matthew Brock Johnson
McKenzie Driggers
Megan Murphy
Misty Humphrey
Mollie Ward
Mollie Hardin
Molly Manella
Monica Huff
Nathan Morgan
Nicole Baker
Olivia Hyer
Olivia Tarvestad
Paris Rippetoe
Patrick Higgins
Patrick Mohr
Phoebe Mclaughlin
Priya Nair
Raelin Enloe

Ramin Gillett
Regan Smith
Richie Ford
Robin Webb
Saida Higgins
Samantha Fry
Samuel Decker
Sara Braca
Sarah Williams
Scarlett Powers
Shelby Goodsell
Sheri Duff
Stephanie Martin
Stephanie Martin
Suzanne McGee
Sydney O'Bryan
Tanner Hoth
Taylor Barnet
Taylor Cianfoni
Taylor Williams
Teri Frazier
Toni Villanueva
Tori Bishop
Tyler Sim
Wendy Smith
Whitney Olsen